Foster Kid *to* Executive

6 Secrets to Building a Successful Tomorrow

Special <u>FREE</u> Bonus Gift for You
To help you to achieve more success, there are
FREE BONUS RESOURCES for you at:

www.mandyfrench.com

Get your Success Toolkit:
including your Dream Catcher, Gratitude Grid,
Paving Your Path, Habit Trackers, and much more.

MANDY FRENCH

mandy french

Foster Kid to Executive: 6 Secrets to Building a Successful Tomorrow
Copyright © 2024 by Mandy French, LLC

All rights reserved. No part of this book may be reproduced or transmitted in any form or by any means without written permission from the author.

Edited by Krista Hoeschen
Cover Design by Stephanie McGowan
Photographs by Gavin Howard

Disclaimer: This book contains opinions, ideas, experiences and exercises. The purchaser and/or reader of these materials assumes all responsibility for the use of this information. Mandy French and Mandy French, LLC assume no responsivity and/or liability whatsoever for any purchaser and reader of these materials.

mandy french
www.mandyfrench.com

Mandy French
www.mandyfrench.com

MOTIVATE & INSPIRE OTHERS

Give the Gift of Success

Paperback Retail $19.99

Special Quantity Discounts

5-20 Books	$17.99
21-99 Books	$15.99
100-499 Books	$13.99
500-999 Books	$11.99
1,000+ Books	$9.99

*Discount pricing subject to change

To place an order visit:
www.mandyfrench.com

THE IDEAL SPEAKER FOR YOUR NEXT EVENT!

Any organization that wants to inspire and develop youth to become "extraordinary," needs to hire Mandy French for a keynote and/or workshop training!

TO CONTACT OR BOOK MANDY FRENCH TO SPEAK VISIT:

www.mandyfrench.com

Mandy French
www.mandyfrench.com

THE IDEAL COACH FOR YOU!

If you're ready to overcome challenges, have major breakthroughs and achieve higher levels, then you will love having Mandy French as your coach!

**TO CONTACT
MANDY FRENCH
VISIT:
www.mandyfrench.com**

I dedicate this book to all the extraordinary and resilient foster youth; may this book be a beacon of light on your path to self-discovery and personal growth. Embrace your potential, navigate challenges with courage, and find the strength within to create a future filled with purpose and fulfillment. *You* determine your destiny - may these words inspire and empower you on your journey.

Table of Contents

Introduction: A Message for You — **9**

Secret 1: Choose to Choose — **19**

Secret 2: Mind Over Matter — **45**

Secret 3: Give It Your All — **61**

Secret 4: Paving the Way — **75**

Secret 5: Don't Do Life Alone — **95**

Secret 6: The Nudge — **111**

One Last Message: Gluing It Together — **121**

About the Author — **131**

Acknowledgments — **133**

Introduction: A Message for You

People begin to become successful the minute they decide to be.
— *Harvey Mackay,*
New York Best Selling Author and Businessman

It was 1993, I was eight years old and had been pestering my mom for days about signing a permission slip for a field trip for my class that I wanted to attend. We were sitting on an old brown couch in our Section 8 housing; it was a gray three-bedroom townhome. We had moved there when my parents got a divorce. My mom brought my two sisters and me from Rockford, Illinois, to Owatonna, Minnesota, to be closer to family. Leading up to this moment, I had watched as my younger sister, and then my older sister was placed into foster care. So, in this moment, I could feel the heaviness in the air as my mom hugged me tightly; it was my turn. I could feel my childhood slowly fading away, making room for the harsh reality of life that infiltrated my very being. It was a heavy, crushing, breaking, cracking sensation that I felt deep in my chest as my heart began to shatter. She told me that she couldn't sign the permission slip because tomorrow a social worker was going to pick me up from school and take me to live at the foster home in which my older sister lived. In that moment, I felt outside of my body, watching events unfold like a movie, as if it was happening to someone else. The truth, my truth, was realizing I could no longer deny what was happening to my family. There was no more pretending to be like everyone else — it was official, I was different. I already didn't have a dad, my sisters were gone, and now I was losing my mom. At only eight years of life, my innocence was gone, and I grew up. My whole being shifted to survival.

The next day I got up, said good-bye to my mom and went to school. The heaviness of my new reality weighed me down. After lunch, two social workers picked me up and walked me to a car parked outside the school. In the car was a small backpack filled with the few belongings I had. It was a 90-minute drive to reach my new home, my new reality, with the unknown hanging in the air. It was both the longest and shortest car ride. The hills felt like mountains as the car carried us up and then down — I wondered, what would the next hill reveal? How could I stop this roller coaster? How can I get back to safety? I didn't want to go, I didn't want to be brave, I didn't want to pretend it didn't matter. As the wheels kept turning, I stared out the window until finally we turned onto a gravel road — a road I would travel thousands of times, riding bikes, taking walks, school bus rides, and the like. I sometimes referred to it as the road to hell, but over time I realized it was a road that led me to the place that would shape my future. A place that built my character, gave me resilience, provided me with perspective, and taught me to choose.

I spent the rest of my childhood in foster care. The first home was a licensed group-home which housed up to 10 kids at a time; many were high-risk, and many were at the last stop before juvenile detention or residential lock up. I have so many stories, so many experiences from that place; all I will say here is, I survived. When I was 17, I was given the option to move to a new home. I did and this choice changed the trajectory of my life. I graduated high school with honors and was awarded a full-ride scholarship to a private liberal arts college. I spent the next four years learning and socializing with "normal" kids, learning how to be a part of their world before graduating with a degree in History in 2007.

Initially, I took a job with Aflac Insurance – it seemed like a great opportunity, so I ventured to an insurance certification class upon graduation. I passed the test and headed into the office expecting to find my cubicle and office supplies ready for me to take on the insurance industry. I was sorely disappointed when I learned that I was on my own.

What? I hadn't understood that this was a commission job. There were lots of opportunities to make money, but you had to provide your own administrative foundation and then start cold calling. Nope, that wasn't for me. I found myself jobless with a small amount of savings and an apartment to pay for which I needed rent. I leaned on my faith: *everything will work out the way it is supposed to*. A few days later, I received an email from the Department of Veterans Affairs (VA) requesting me to come in for an interview. I didn't know anything about working for the government. I certainly didn't know anything about the Veterans Benefits Administration, but I did know I needed a job and the va.gov email address it came from seemed legit. I accepted the interview. A week later, I went to the office and walked out with a job as a claim's processor.

Shortly thereafter, I was placed on a special project allowing me to take on informal leadership positions, mentoring, training, and coming up with suggestions for making our operations more consistent and functional. I quickly found myself on a leadership trajectory at work. While the work was gratifying, being a claims processor wasn't my calling. My calling was working with people. I loved training and helping others learn the process and find confidence in their work. Working at the VA was very gratifying; serving Veterans, their families and caregivers coupled with the ability to help others gave me purpose. By focusing on doing my best in my current role, I was promoted to a front-line leader. I was extremely ambitious and open to the universe telling me what my next steps were. It wasn't long after that when a mentor of mine tapped me on the shoulder and suggested that I apply for a training consultant position in headquarters. *Why not?* The worst someone could say was no and it seemed that life was nudging me to apply for this job. The VA Headquarters is located in Washington,

D.C. and if I got the job, they would pay for my relocation. As I considered it, I realized I didn't have a lot keeping me in Minnesota and someone told me once that I should be prepared to work at the headquarters of any job I accepted. So, I submitted the job application and a few months later was selected.

Once again, the comfort and familiarity of my life was about to change; a new chapter was about to begin. I spent the next four and half years in D.C., I continued to work my way up and managed to achieve GS14, making six figures before I was 30. (Federal employee salaries are determined by the General Schedule, GS, which has grades from 1-15.) I made my career a priority and my hard work was paying off. In many ways, I was figuring out how to navigate the professional world and build a career. I was honing my leadership skills and the ability to work through others. I believe in leading through influence, not power.

Despite this success, I realized I was living to work instead of working to live. My social life was made up of work colleagues, my priorities were on anything but myself, and after four and half years, I felt life's nudges; it was time for a change. Working in headquarters taught me a lot about the organization, it also taught me a lot about leadership and enabled me to build a brand. I felt compelled to reconnect with the foundation of the organization, which was serving Veterans and serving the employees that were on the ground making the decisions and working to fulfill the mission. So, I consulted with Tux, my cat, and we made a list of all the places we would be willing to move. *Kidding, it was me, but he seemed "all in" on the decision.* It was just the two of us with a map of the country and opportunity awaiting.

Salt Lake City would be our next stop; I had gone there for a site visit the year before and the city was incredible with its massive mountains taking up the horizon on both sides of the valley. I could imagine us living in such a beautiful place. I applied for an Assistant Veterans Service Center Manager (AVSCM) position and was selected. Once more, I found myself zigzagging across the country to start a new chapter. I loved the small town feel with all the big city amenities Salt Lake City had to offer. I had just turned 30 years old and as I was transitioning to my new locale, I vowed to make some changes: bring balance to my life and take care of me. Also, eating well, taking care of my body, and making healthy choices that would fulfill my mental and physical health goals – all things I hadn't really been taught as a kid.

Amid all these aspirations, I met the man who would become my husband and quickly what I thought would be a steppingstone became a landing pad. He had two daughters from a prior marriage who were in high school, so I decided to settle in and buy my first house. I was lucky to have the ability to take out a loan against my Thrift Savings Plan (which is a retirement savings plan for Federal employees, like a 401(k) in the private sector) to use as the down payment. Buying a home is hard when you don't have help, but oh does it feel good when you can do it all by yourself!

I spent a little over four years as an AVSCM. When the manager in our Fiduciary department left, it opened an opportunity for promotion and growth. I applied for the position, interviewed for it twice and ended up leaving my AVSCM position for maternity leave. I came back to work in a new role: Fiduciary Hub Manager. This was another tough job and learning to balance this with my new-found motherhood wasn't an easy task. As you might have realized by now though, taking on a challenge is what I love most doing. The Hub needed a lot of work; it needed structure and training, and it needed leadership. Over the course of the next few years I, alongside an amazing team, brought the Hub to the next level.

By this time my husband, Jim, and I had gotten married and his two daughters from his prior marriage had graduated from high school. I found myself considering an executive position as assistant director which would relocate our family. We decided to put my name in the ring for two opportunities. One in St. Petersburg, Florida; this would bring us closer to Jim's brother and with my daughter, Evelyn, being just over 3 years old at the time, having family close by was very appealing. The second was in Phoenix, Arizona, and after some encouragement from colleagues and soul-searching, I was quickly offered the position in Phoenix and took it. Holy smokes, I was barely 37 and I had gone from foster kid to executive in less than 15 years.

And that leads me to today. I find myself reflecting on the first half of my life and trying to figure out what I want to do with the second half. I have built an incredible career, had unimaginable success, and am blessed with a beautiful family. How is it possible that the little girl who was placed in foster care at the age of eight, aging out of the system a decade later, has been able to build this incredible life? The odds were not in my favor and if you do a simple online search, you will find that for a kid aging out of foster care, the future is bleak. Seventy percent become pregnant before the age of 21; 20% become instantly homeless; 60% end up in the sex-trade industry; less than 3% get a college degree at any time in their life. It is a miracle that I have been able to leave the system and be as successful as I am.

So how did I do it, and how do you replicate it? I've been asked over and over, "what's the secret sauce?" And after much prayer and reflection, it is not an equation or a singular moment. It isn't just grit and perseverance; it's a mindset and it is faith. It's about making your own path when the odds say you can't. It takes commitment and action. There is no room for complacency and zero room for excuses. In fact, it is about pushing through your past, letting go of the things you can't control and focusing on the things you can. Seeing the future for what it can be and making choices today that will make tomorrow easier.

In the following secrets to success, I am going to share tools that you can use for a better tomorrow. As a kid, there is so much out of your control; you don't choose your parents or siblings, you don't choose where you live, the school you go to, the community you live in, you don't choose the family you've been placed with. It feels so unfair. I remember sitting at the edge of a corn field, in the first few months of being placed into to foster care, crying out to God, "why me, why am I here, why…" tears streaming down my face, anguish in my heart, pity for myself and the situation in which I found myself. When suddenly, a huge turkey vulture flew out of the corn field, soaring just feet over my head. I gazed at its giant wingspan sprawling above me. I sat there stunned, scared, and quietly wiping my tears, unsure what God was trying to tell me. I walked away that day and never asked God why again. I'm not sure if He was trying to tell me to quit feeling sorry for myself or if He was trying to tell me that every being on earth has a purpose and a path. What I do know, is that in that moment, I made a choice to not look back but to look forward.

Although it feels like today is forever, it is only today. Tomorrow will come and what you do today shapes the opportunities that will allow you to succeed tomorrow.

Secret *One*

CHOOSE TO CHOOSE

Choices, not circumstances, determine your success.
— Unknown

What you need to understand is that life is a series of choices. We make choices and those choices, whether big or small, dictate the direction and outcome of our lives. Each choice has a cascading effect on our lives. What I have learned is most people, especially youth, do not see the connection between the decisions and choices they make today and the outcomes they experience tomorrow. If you can master the art of choosing, the odds of your life moving in the right direction are exponentially increased.

It's hard to see past *today* when you're a kid, even more so when you are just trying to survive, but the ability to do so will only make life easier later. People ask me if I would change my circumstances: I was eight years old when I entered foster care, an age at which I could have still been adopted out, but my mom didn't want to give up her rights as a parent. This left me growing up in the system exposed to the chaos, uncertainty, and challenges that come along with being in that situation. The answer is no, I wouldn't change anything. It has made me who I am and, in many ways, stronger and more resilient than those without my experience. Throughout it all, it's the choices I made growing up in foster care that have led me to a life of opportunity, success, love, and fulfillment.

We live in a country where you can grow up poor, in the system, and you can rise above your circumstances, to accomplish whatever you want. This is the beauty of America and what you do today can allow you to create the life you want tomorrow. Maybe it's a life that is financially and emotionally stable, a life where you can give your future family everything you didn't have, or maybe, it's something else. Do not let anyone tell you differently, the American Dream is alive and well — but it isn't going to be given to you. You must earn it; you must put in the effort and make the decisions that will allow you to climb the social and economic ladders of society.

Does it ever feel like we live in a culture of excuses about why you can't rise above your circumstances? People are going to put labels on you and tell you why you can't do it. They'll say you're not smart enough, don't come from the right family, or you live on the wrong side of the tracks. DO NOT LISTEN! Do not let anyone tell you what you can't do — because you can, through the power of choice. You must learn to make choices that will prepare you for the right opportunities. If you let someone else choose, or you're sitting back and waiting for success to come to you or expecting some kind of magic success pill to appear, not only will you be waiting a long time, but you likely will not see a change in your circumstances. You will be stuck in the same life you have always known, struggling through adulthood, and possibly putting your own kids in a similar situation in which you found yourself at the same age. Or something worse, you become homeless, addicted to drugs, selling the only thing you have, your body. DO NOT become another statistic.

Poverty and social status are generational; meaning, if you grow up in a poor household, there's a likely chance you will have the same socioeconomic challenges as an adult. However, you have the ability to make the choices to break this cycle. It starts today and it starts by taking control of your life now and not letting the people and circumstances around you dictate who you are and how you behave.

My high school teacher, Mr. Marshall, once said to me, "Mandy, remember to choose because not choosing is also a choice." This really stuck with me, and it couldn't be truer. As a kid you feel powerless, especially when you have bounced around the system. It feels like no one cares and that everything is out of your control. It's easy to let things happen to you, and not make deliberate choices – only focusing on the things you cannot control. But there are choices, there are always choices.

Small choices make a big difference.

When I was a kid, I decided to be a lawyer when I grew up. I remember declaring this at a very early age and it acted as a lighthouse for me, a beacon of light. It helped me guide the decisions I made as I grew up. I began making choices that would allow me to achieve this goal: I chose to do my homework, to show up, and put effort into school. I allowed teachers, coaches, and pastors to mentor me and guide me. I surrounded myself with other kids who were smart and like-minded. Each small choice I made that supported this goal and got me one step closer to escaping my circumstances.

Looking forward to my senior year of high school and all the effort I put into school. The choices to learn, develop, and grow allowed me to win a full scholarship to a private college. Consider what might have happened if I hadn't made this commitment. What if I blew off school, didn't do my homework, made excuses for why I wasn't smart enough, or didn't care enough? The opportunity to get a free education would not have existed. You must make choices today so that tomorrow you are prepared for what new opportunities may arise to get you one step closer to your goal.

There are four elements to making good choices; 1. Have a vision of your future – DREAM BIG; 2. Understand what you control – sphere of control; 3. Have delayed gratification; 4. Review your choices and adjust for better outcomes.

Dream Big

Take a minute and close your eyes. I want you to imagine the perfect life, *your* perfect life. How does it look in your 20's, and then in your 30's? Where do you live? What is your job? Do you have a family? How much money do you make? What kind of car do you drive? Who are you with? What does your lifestyle look like? How does your future self-feel? Take some time to reflect on what this means to you, don't hold back, DREAM. Use the lines below to write down what you are picturing. Be specific. You may also visit www.mandyfrench.com/free-gift to access the Success Toolbox and complete the *Dream-Catcher* worksheet.

_____

_____

_____

_____

_____

_____

_____

_____

Mandy French
www.mandyfrench.com

Foster Kid to Executive
6 Secrets to a Successful Tomorrow

Mandy French
www.mandyfrench.com

Mandy French
www.mandyfrench.com

Foster Kid to Executive
6 Secrets to a Successful Tomorrow

Mandy French
www.mandyfrench.com

I imagine your perfect life didn't include addiction, welfare, anxiety, fear, poverty, homelessness, entrapment, abandonment, hurt, or pain. You likely are imagining a life free of these struggles, many of which you might be experiencing today. Did you imagine freedom from the circumstances that surround you? An easier life where you can afford luxuries, experience happiness through your relationships and achievements? Maybe you're in a big city high-rise taking the metro to work, you live in the country with a garden and house full of kids, or something else altogether. No matter what your vision for the future is—have a vision. Don't let the heaviness and gravity of today keep you from dreaming big.

Now let's think of this dream as your long-term goal for a life that is different from today. It's time to plan how you're going to get there. Remember, a goal without a plan is just a dream. Don't let each day slip by without making a deliberate choice to move another step closer to creating the reality you've imagined – even if it's just one choice, commit to it.

What are the choices you are currently making? Do these choices lead you to that dream or not? Do they give you satisfaction in the moment, not setting you up for opportunities later? Easy is not always better; understand that there are consequences, good and bad, for every choice we make. Will the ripple effects of your decisions get you closer to escaping today's reality or will they keep you trapped – close to a lifestyle of poverty, crime, and addiction? The hard choices of today *will* lead to an easier tomorrow.

So, you now have a vision. You've set in motion a goal to create a better life for yourself – incredible. You can imagine it, see it, feel it, touch it, you can almost taste it. Keep going. Consider the feeling when you realize your dream? You might be thinking; great, now, how do I get there? What can I do to control my circumstances?

Sphere of Control

It feels like you have no control, all these things have happened to you. If you had chosen, you would have imagined something so much better. A place of love and happiness, a place of support, a place where you blend in, where you are normal – essentially the flipside of all those negative labels you experience in the system. Maybe it's a place where people see all your potential and life comes easy – where you're not worried about your next meal, what home or family you'll live with, how people are judging you for not being like them. You didn't choose this life and there is nothing you can do to change the circumstances that brought you to this moment.

The first lesson in understanding your sphere of control is understanding you do not have the ability to change the past. There is absolutely nothing you can do; what is done is done. Stop looking back; focus on what you can do now to create the future you imagine for yourself tomorrow. Even though you might have made poor choices or fell into the trap of choosing not to choose (which is still a choice) you can change course. You always have the choice to take a different path and only you can make that choice for yourself. There is no one who can (or will) do it for you. You are the leader of your own life. Own it!

Perhaps you're saying, *well, that's great but there isn't a whole lot in my control now either*. There is. You control your mindset (we'll explore this more in the next secret), you control the decision about your friends and people you associate with, you control the way you react to the circumstances around you, and you control the effort you put into your activities and learning. Always remember, knowledge is power.

Stop for a moment and consider the people with whom you are associating. Do they raise you up and make you a better person or are they encouraging poor decisions? Are they leading you down the wrong path? Who you associate with will determine the types of decisions you make. Keep your circle small and level up —surround yourself with the type of people you admire. If you're hanging with a crowd that pressures you to make choices that lead you away from your vision, one day you will wake up and realize you haven't moved forward, you're stuck. You control who your friends are, choose wisely.

Take some time, using the diagram on the next page to capture what is in your sphere of control and what is outside your sphere of control. You may also visit www.mandyfrench.com/free-gift to access the Success Toolbox and complete the *Taking Control* worksheet.

Out of Your Control

In Your Control

The last piece of sphere of control is understanding cause and effect. My foster mom never used the word punishment; it was always a consequence for our actions. She wanted us to understand the cause and effect of the decisions we made. If the choices we made were against the rules, there were consequences for our actions. It became very clear, very fast (at least for me) that I wanted to avoid negative consequences.

Pro tip: Use consequences as a guide. There is nothing wrong with making mistakes, we all do. The key is learning from them. If every time you go down a certain path a snake slithers out and bites you, why would you continue taking that path? Ask yourself if the choice that led you to that path supports your vision of the future. Are there adjustments you need to make to ensure the path you are on is leading to the future you've set out for yourself? What do you have in your sphere of control to change the direction you're going?

When you take the wrong path, it is imperative to reflect on how you got there and what you have learned from the experience. Put the results in your toolbox and move on. Know you're going to make a better choice next time. Actions have consequences, and the choices you make will impact the gravity of those consequences. You can't dwell on a mistake or a bad choice; lamenting on what you've done is not helpful. Instead, analyze the situation, understand your role, and what you can do differently in the future that fits in your sphere of control. I call this a mental after-action report.

Although I am telling you to learn from your mistakes and move on, I want you to recognize the consequences of your actions can have far reaching effects. If you are on a path of destruction and the choices you are making continue to compound – stealing, drugs, alcohol abuse, violence —the consequences of these choices can have lasting effects on your future. The whole point of this is to stop the path of destruction before it gets to that point.

If you have already made decisions that led to consequences which will have lasting impacts on your future, I want you to know that it is never too late to course correct. It may be harder, and you may have to sacrifice a lot to get back on track, but you can do it— you're the only one who can. You are the leader of your life, and no one can make choices for you. Look at your sphere of control and start making the right choices today, your future self will thank you.

Delayed Gratification

For the choices that serve fulfilling your vision you must embrace delayed gratification. This starts with thinking before acting. Impulsive choices lead to unpredictable and sometimes poor consequences. This can compound and lead you away from your vision. So, as I talk about delayed gratification and why and how it is so important in all areas of your life, I want you to learn to be intentional in how you choose. Take 30 seconds, five minutes, a full day —however long it takes to think through the decisions you are making that can have lasting effects on your future.

If you find yourself in a place where you can't take that moment to process the consequences of the decision you are making, walk away. It is likely a decision you don't want to make, or it is a decision you are being pressured to make – these impulses typically won't have a favorable outcome for you. It will be difficult, I know. There are so many things that give us instant gratification.

Let's talk more about it. Pretend you're 17, out with a group of friends at a party and there's alcohol; your best friend leans over and hands you a beer. This is the moment when you must train your mind to stop. What could happen if you drink it? Where is it leading you? You think, *well, it's only one. What is my friend going to think if I say no? Saying no would be uncool, people will judge me.* Remember poor choices compound. When you allow yourself to make one bad choice it becomes easier to make another, and another, and another. One beer today might equal two tomorrow, and a 12-pack down the road. This scenario is particularly important if you have alcoholism in your family. Choosing to drink is like playing with fire; don't even put yourself in this space. Masking your hurt or feelings with choices like alcohol and drugs will not make your life better tomorrow. It will cause more hardship, more challenges, and more issues, instead of creating the person you want to be. Don't let the generational bonds of your family entrap you.

I realize everyone's situation is different, so think about your situation. Are there activities, people, places that you should avoid? Thinking back to the party and your hypothetical choices around alcohol, what if that person was your parent or guardian, an uncle or aunt, or your grandparent. The struggle with alcohol is real for many people. Think about how you feel when you see them drink five, six, seven, or 15 beers — how are they acting? Is this what you want for your future self? Is this what you want for your future children? Be strong. Make the hard choice and embrace delayed gratification.

I know impulsive choices in social settings might feel good in the moment. They might fulfill your need to be included, or loved – to escape today's reality, but I plead with you to say no today, so that tomorrow you can be a different person. Your discomfort in not conforming, feeling judged, or left out is short term. And let's be honest, if you are choosing the right people with whom to associate, you shouldn't be judged, ridiculed, or pressured to do something you don't want to do. Remember, you make your own choices, no one else can do that. Choose wisely.

By taking a moment to think through consequences before actions, it will ground you in your values and will help you build the character you need to succeed. Get comfortable with being uncomfortable – over time, new opportunities will present themselves and you can move forward. I mentioned earlier that I received a full ride scholarship to a private liberal arts college. If I had not made the right choices to do my homework, exert effort in school, make the decision to learn and succeed, I wouldn't have been given this blessing. Have faith that the tough choices you are making today are an investment in your future. Don't miss opportunities because you are unwilling to make the hard choices now or unwilling to put the effort into preparing for future opportunities. Rest assured there are opportunities out there, but they aren't going to present themselves if you are not making the right choices now to prepare yourself.

I'm not going to sugarcoat this, yes, people will judge you sometimes. At first, you may be uncomfortable making decisions that will delay your gratification, vs. experiencing satisfaction in the moment. But we are talking about ways to give you a different, better life in the future – it's worth it, trust me. Choices you make will lead you to your vision, your dream, your ability to break the chains that hold you back. Make choices now to protect your future self, your future family, and build the foundation you need to succeed.

Mental After-Action Review

Believe me when I say I've made a lot of poor choices in my life, and I can count myself lucky that some of those decisions didn't ruin my future. I thank God for protecting me and giving me the opportunity to learn from those mistakes without ruining my future. This is the key; taking each poor choice as an opportunity to learn.

So, what is a mental after-action review? Just as we discussed the importance of taking time *before* making a choice to think through the possible impacts and repercussions, a mental after-action review is doing the same thing *after* making a choice and realizing the outcome. This allows you to have a clear understanding of the cause and effect of your decisions. Consider, what was the outcome, and did it have the intended effect you thought about before making the choice? Is it a choice you should make again, or are there some adjustments you can make next time? Recognize how you can do things differently in the future.

I would recommend keeping yourself open when reflecting on outcomes and not looking through a negative, consequential lens. Take time to reflect when things go well also. Your goal always is to replicate the good choices you are making —the choices that are making your life easier or resulting in opportunities. This will take practice – stick with it. When things don't go well, it is important to make sure you learn from the situation and put steps in place to adjust your approach for a different outcome. Remember, you can't keep doing the same things and expect different results.

When doing a mental after-action review, I want you to remember the acronym SAR:

> **Situation** – What happened?
> **Action** – What choice did you make? What role did you play?
> **Result** – What happened? What went well; what didn't? What could you do differently?

I encourage you to take some time each day, using the above format to journal and reflect on outcomes. This will give you a clear understanding of the cause and effect of your choices, actions, and experiences.

Let's practice; think of a choice you've recently made and do a mental after-action review using SAR (use the lines below). You may also visit www.mandyfrench.com/free-gift to access the Success Toolbox and complete the *Thinking it Through: SAR Worksheet.*

Situation:_____

_____

_____

_____

_____

_____

Action:_____

_____

Result:_____

_____

Before closing this secret, I hope you take a moment to reflect on the value of who you are and how much you can do in the now to control your future circumstances. I know it is hard to envision the future without the hurt, anger, and loneliness you may be feeling right now, but you are worth it. Focus on your vision (we will discuss more about goal setting later – these are the tangible milestones you can set to reach your dreams.) Let the circumstances of today be *why* you are going to make choices today that will bear fruit tomorrow. I promise that today is temporary and your investment in yourself will pay off!

Choose to choose.

Mandy French
www.mandyfrench.com

Secret *Two*

MIND OVER MATTER

The mind is everything; what you think you become.
– *Buddha, Spiritual Leader*

Mindset: the established set of *attitudes* held by someone.

We discussed sphere of control in the last secret, and I want to dive into this concept in relation to mindset. In my introduction, I talked about many of the things that are outside of your control, the things you don't choose. These are often external variables: places you must be, like school, where you are from, where you live now, and the adults in your life (your birth parents, social workers, guardians, and foster parents) — these are all things you can't control. So, what do you control? Your attitude and how you respond to the people around you. You control the activities you participate in and how much effort you put into them. Focusing on the things you control will help move your energy in a positive direction.

I recommend spending 90% of your energy on the things you can control and 10% of your energy influencing the people and things outside of your control. Influencing is convincing others of your point of view. In taking this approach, the effort you exert will be for *your* benefit. If all your time and energy is spent on things outside of your control you will feel powerless and stuck; instead focus on what you *can* do to move yourself forward.

Now, let's take it one step further. Consider some of your negative experiences; it might include emotional, financial, physical or sexual abuse. It may be abandonment or drug abuse. You may be the caretaker for your siblings or live with hunger and daily challenges to nourish your body. Perhaps it's homelessness, living in filth, or things you never want anyone else to know about. It's likely that someone, at some point, challenged your self-worth by saying you're not good enough or smart enough. They might have told you how bad you are, how much you've failed, how you will never amount to anything, or how you're just a foster kid with issues. People placed these labels on you and maybe you've believed them, putting these labels on yourself. Not only are labels like this negative, but they are also limiting, and they produce destructive self-talk. They become self-fulfilling prophecies. I'm here to remind you that no one can limit your capabilities. Remember to focus on the things within your control—your mindset.

It is human nature to compare ourselves to others, to look at the circumstances of others and perceive their lives as being better in some way or "normal". Sometimes this makes us see ourselves as victims, pitying ourselves and blaming others for our circumstances. What if you're not a victim? What if the experiences you have gone through gave you something unique, something that is very difficult to get any other way? The gift you have been given is resiliency. You are capable of overcoming adversity, shedding those negative labels, and learning from your experiences – bouncing back from the challenges you have experienced. It's your life, and you can control what happens next. Take these challenges and turn them into gifts. You must believe that you can be, and do, anything you want. You can overcome your limitations and learn to recognize opportunity and set yourself up for success. No one can do it for you, only you can *choose* to take on a mindset that will allow you to succeed. You must believe in yourself.

In fact, my journey has uncovered that kids who grow up without adversity and challenges tend to struggle with everyday life in adulthood. I know it is hard to understand and appreciate now, but the challenges you are experiencing today are giving you tools that so many others don't have, tools that give you a leg up on being successful later. Consider the skills you are learning and apply them to the choices you make today. It starts with your mindset.

Mindset is categorized in two ways, people with a fixed mindset and people with a growth mindset.

According to the leading psychologist on mindset, Carol Dweck, Ph.D., fixed mindset is someone who thinks that the labels, personality, abilities, strengths, and weaknesses of a person are set. In short, what you were born with is what you've got. This is a very black and white perspective which limits people from striving to develop new skills. In fact, this is the way most of our society functions; being complacent with what is happening to you. We are trained from an early age to recognize our traits and abilities (good and bad) which will determine our success. This is NOT the mindset for you.

A growth mindset is believing you can (continuously) develop yourself through dedication and hard work. It starts with your values and commitment to the idea that anything you put your mind to you can do. Ability is only one piece of the puzzle. Remember the story about the tortoise and the hare? The hare seemed to have all the abilities to win the race; he's fast, strong, has everyone's support, they believe in him, a natural champion for this challenge. (I can't help but think of those who come from wealthy families with lots of privilege and opportunities – you know, one of the "normal" ones.) And yet, in the end, despite the hare's advantages and abilities, he didn't put in the effort, and he lost the race. On the other hand, the tortoise is slow by comparison, he carries a huge weight on his back. He had few (if any) supporters to cheer him on… He trudged along, doing his best and staying focused. It paid off. (Perhaps he came from a poor family, with few resources and no privilege – you know, one of "those" kids). Despite being slow, the tortoise identified the *opportunity* to race the rabbit. He didn't limit himself by saying, "No, I can't. I'm too slow and carry too much weight." Or "I don't know how to run fast." Instead, he said, "Yes."; willing to try despite the odds. Changing his mindset from I can *try*, to I *can*, to I *will* do it! Imagine what crossing the finish line to your goals will feel like? Take the "race" one step at a time, stay positive, learn as you go, focus, and keep going. See past the labels put on you, dream big, and commit. You can persevere and champion your own life – don't let the abilities and opinions of others impact the choices you make. Anything is possible if you put your mind to it.

Labels Are Only for Jars

How do you become more like the tortoise? The first step is getting past you. What I mean, is getting past the labels that you and others have placed on yourself. You must believe in yourself and your potential to be whatever you want. You *can* grow and change. Don't let others or your own mind limit your abilities.

We had a swing set made of wood that was placed at the end of my foster family's yard. One day I was out there with one of the other foster girls, we were probably 11 or 12 years old, and my foster mom's biological son came up to us and said, "Well, you're just a foster kid." I don't fully remember what prompted him to say that, but he said it in a demeaning way. It was meant to hurt us. It sent a message that we weren't good enough and our circumstances were somehow worse than his. We started pumping our legs and swinging higher. I replied, "I'm not a jar, you can't label me! I'm much more than *just* a foster kid." The girl next to me chimed in and we started shouting out all the things we were, all the value we brought. I felt so much power at that moment. Flying above the circumstances in which I was placed, above the rows of corn, and reaching to the sky. We didn't let him determine our worth or let his label make us feel less than who we were. In fact, we denied him that power. We took control and had the upper hand because we believed in ourselves. And the truth is, he was wrong.

Looking back, this was such a powerful moment. A moment where I didn't allow someone else to define me. You too can take back your power from those around you who expect to see you fail, those who only see you for the labels they've placed on you. Take back your power. With hard work, a growth mindset, and learning from your experiences, you can continue to grow, increase your abilities and then, the sky's the limit. Dream big, because you *can* overcome the labels, the stereotypes, the hurt that others want you to feel.

I'm all about action – we can talk about putting the labels away and seeing ourselves in a new light, but unless we act and truly believe, it won't happen. I want you to use the below listed columns (on the next page). In column A, write down the labels and stereotypes that you feel have been put on you. Use words that describe the fixed view of who you are. In column B, write down words that describe who you want to become based on your dreams (not your circumstances). Column B is the vision of who you are becoming and the shift in your mindset about yourself and your circumstances. This exercise isn't easy and if you're having a hard time, I recommend using "I AM" statements in your growth mindset column. For example: I am strong and resilient, I am beautiful, I am capable of loving and being loved, I am smart, I am independent, I am capable, I am worthy, and so on. You may also visit www.mandyfrench.com/free-gift to access the Success Toolbox and complete the *Mind Over Matter* worksheet.

A Fixed Mindset	B Growth Mindset

Glass Half-Full — Attitude is Everything

Another part of having a growth mindset is looking at life through a positive lens. As we discussed, eliminating negative labels starts with viewing yourself in a positive light, but it goes beyond just your self-image and self-talk. This intention must carry into everything you do. Being optimistic doesn't mean that you don't recognize the negative things in life, or that there isn't pessimism in the world, but it puts you back in control of the situation. If you can see the best in every person and every situation you will have a much better chance of learning from the situation, building resiliency, and drawing positivity towards you. Let me be clear, I understand that it is difficult to have a positive outlook when sometimes it feels like everything is going wrong. What I need you to realize is optimism is powerful. Do you see the glass half-full or half-empty? In both instances, the glass has the same amount of water, it's just how you perceive it. It is difficult to have a positive life if you are always negative. If you can learn to analyze every situation and frame it in a positive light, I promise, you'll be a happier person. Positive thinking leads to positive outcomes. There is always a silver lining and an opportunity to learn. Don't believe every stupid thing your mind says to you.

In the words of Forest Gump — sometimes, (sh)IT happens — because it does, and when it happens, are you going to wallow in IT? By focusing on negativity and how you've been wronged or let down, you are letting others control your outlook. This impacts your attitude and often you'll become angry, lose your temper, or lose control. In short, they win, and you lose – every time. Take that pause and breathe deep. Learn from the situation, remember the after-action review? (Reflect on the situation, your action, and the result.) Over time, you'll build resiliency to life's unpredictable challenges and maintain control. With experience, you'll be able to learn from these situations and move on with a positive attitude. Don't let other people dictate how you feel and how you act. Understand that the only person you can control is you.

When life feels overwhelming, and things aren't going your way, there is one thing over which you always have control, your attitude. Your attitude is power. Just the simple act of putting a smile on your face makes a huge difference. How you feel affects how you function. Take some time in every challenging situation to reframe what is happening and look for silver linings. There is an opportunity for growth if you consider what you can learn from the circumstance.

I was talking to someone the other day and they said to me, "Mandy, you may not have been born with a silver spoon, but you were born with a happy one!" This made me chuckle because it is truly my philosophy, I apply it to everything I do. Not only does a positive approach help me, but it also impacts the people around me. Positivity draws positivity; when you're viewing life from the *glass half-full* perspective you make better choices, you grow, and you attract people who want to help you succeed. It's the ability to take the negative and flip it around to benefit you. Consider what you can get out of a situation and capitalize on it.

Just as positive draws positive, negative draws negative. Think about the everyday things you are doing that do not support positivity. Think about the music you are listening to and the friends you are hanging out with each day. If these things are negative, they *will* infiltrate your thoughts and your actions. It is like a slow growing mold in your mind — this negativity will permeate, just like the labels others have put on you, you will start believing them. Instead feed your mind and soul with positivity; surround yourself with the things that will uplift you and elevate your life, not drag it down. I challenge you to start each day by writing down three things you are grateful for and three things about which you are excited. This may be hard at first, you may feel like there is nothing to be grateful for, but I promise you, you can find something. It may be as simple as being grateful for the sunshine or spring rain. You may be grateful for the relationships in your life, or the kind words of a stranger from the previous day. Whatever it is, no matter how small, expressing this gratitude will set your day up for success. Make today the *best day yet*. Be excited for what may unfold and the opportunities that may present themselves. Take control.

Journaling your negative thoughts and impulses is a tool you can use to better understand how your mind works and when to focus more on the positive. First, start with what you are saying to yourself that isn't positive. What are the negative thoughts? What self-talk do you have that is not encouraging and positive? Write it down; write down the time of day, what you have eaten, who you have interacted with, the music to which you've been listening. Reflect on the environment you are in when you start hearing the negativity seep into your thoughts. You can do this for your negative thoughts, but also your negative impulses. For example, when you get angry with someone or find yourself acting out, think about who you are with and what is happening and why. Take time to look at when this is happening. Are there common threads of people, places, or things that take you to these dark, negative places? Now, reflect on the spaces where you feel positive or have more self-control. These are the things that counteract negativity and will help you with positive affirmations, supportive people, uplifting places, and things to help you grow. Visit www.mandyfrench.com/free-gift to access the Success Toolbox and download the *Pinpoint Journal*.

Finally, I want to encourage you to *get up and show up* – present yourself according to how you want to be treated. This doesn't mean you are putting on designer clothes and going out rockstar style every day, but it does mean you should get dressed and take pride in what you look like. How you dress and how you present yourself establishes your brand. We live in a world where people *will* judge you based on how you look. If your pants are halfway down to your knees or you are wearing offensive clothing, just know that people will not *see you*, they are going to see what you are wearing. They are going to judge you. I don't want to discourage you from expressing yourself or being creative, but I need you to understand that this affects how people perceive and treat you. Part of success is understanding how people view you and helping others have confidence in who you are. Making good decisions about how you present yourself will often determine whether (or not) someone thinks you fit into their definition of success and whether they are going to invest an opportunity in you. Don't limit yourself by not allowing people to see you for who you are. This is a choice, so understand how it effects how you are perceived and what opportunities may come your way based on those perceptions.

As you transition into the working world, I can't tell you how important it is for you to maintain a positive growth mindset and confident brand. As the old saying goes, dress for the job you want, not the job you have. Even in this virtual and remote world, it is easy to let professionalism go because you're not really "seeing" anyone. But you see yourself and you will 100% act more professionally, think more positively, and be more productive if you dress for the job. So, put the yoga pants away and show up for the job you want! If you can go into the office – do it, there is more opportunity to interact, network, and have impact if you are a part of the work culture and not just checking the box and doing the bare minimum. Be engaged.

Knowledge is Power

Don't let anyone tell you you're not smart enough or don't have the ability to do something. Learning, skills, and abilities are not set. You can do anything you set your mind to; it just takes work. You must be committed and never satisfied with the status quo. Be a life-long learner.

As a kid, like many of you, I wanted to escape my reality and be somewhere else. I found this escape in books. For years, I would read book after book after book — taking my mind off my situation and transcending me into worlds of magic, romance, mystery, and drama. It was a way for me to not only escape but it taught me about different ways of living. It exposed me to what I wanted to be and the life I wanted to live. It gave me a place to dream and imagine. Reading gave me hope that I too could live a magical life, that I had the ability to create it here and now. I also learned more, increased my vocabulary, and became more articulate. It helped me be more creative in my life and gave me perspective — it made me smarter and become a critical thinker.

In a world encompassed with screens, enticing video reels, and a plethora of information at our fingertips, the art of reading is quickly becoming a lost pastime. Don't let the opportunity to find new worlds and explore new places in the written word be lost to you. Use this tool to better your mind, train it, and fill it with knowledge and perspective. Let it give you hope and make you smarter. Never stop learning. Beyond books you can learn anything you set your mind to. Yes, some people have a strong, natural ability when it comes to reading, but repetition and dedication to learning will set you apart. You can, and will, pass by others if you stay at it – just like the tortoise and the hare. Take pride in what you do and don't limit yourself. Find what interests you and build that skill.

Ask yourself what you do with all your free time. If it's spent in front of YouTube or TikTok, zoning out watching what others do, I challenge you to use your free time in a way that will build your skills, increase your brain power, and help yourself be a better version of you. Something I've learned to do as an adult, is use my commute time to listen to audio books. It's my *mobile university* and it allows me to use space in my day that would typically be taken up listening to music and transitioning it to a time to build my bank of knowledge and learn new things. It keeps me focused on continuous improvement and ensures I'm not complacent with what I know but am always challenging myself to know more. I challenge you to do the same, whether that be through reading books, listening to books, or informative podcasts, be a life-long learner.

I can't overstate the importance of education. If you take away anything from me, take away that I am telling you to take your education seriously. Intelligence must be cultivated, and your future depends on your ability to learn and prepare yourself for the next chapter in your life. Education is the springboard to opportunity. Many of you may not have someone pushing you to get good grades or making you sit down to do your homework, but you must have the discipline to do these things; they will prepare you for opportunity later. Education gives you the tools to rise above your situation and gives you credibility in a world that values intelligence and knowledge. You can be the best singer, artist, or engineer, but if you can't speak to others or critically think, it will be difficult for you to be successful in the industry of which you dream of being a part of. Education is your foundation, and it will help guide you to your next step. The ability to take this seriously will likely determine how quickly you can overcome your circumstances and guide the opportunities available to you.

There is book smart and there is street smart. Having the combination of both will make you unstoppable. Formal education ensures you can read, write, do math, and provides the foundational skills to do life, but you also need to have common sense. Common sense is the ability to understand people and situations that happen and to make sound judgment calls. Learning outside of the classroom is about taking every situation you encounter and understanding what lesson life is trying to teach you.

As a kid from a non-traditional family, having a mom who was mentally ill, no father figure, living in a foster home where 'crazy' was the norm, I was exposed to trauma, mental illness, and forced to overcome immense adversity. At the same time, I was given the opportunity to experience life early on in the game. You have been given the same opportunity. What I mean is, you have been put into situations at such a young age that it provides you with the street smarts to survive, to be a creative problem solver, and to think outside the box. These are skills not everyone has, and you have them. This is why your after-action reviews are so important, they help you develop your life's journey where you want it to go. You must take the time to recognize the lessons you're learning and to which you have been exposed. Not just letting life happen to you but leading the life you've been given. So, take the time to do those after-action reviews and find the silver linings to ensure you recognize where to adjust, and be better prepared for the next situation. Adversity is a gift if you can learn from it and use it to help you get through another season. Remember, you're building skills that will benefit you later.

I've often been asked if I could change my past, and could have grown up in a "normal" household, with loving parents and "all the things", would I change it? No. I wouldn't do it over again; my past helped me build the character and resilience I have today- my silver lining. I learned so much about what life is and what life isn't through the experiences and relationships of so many during that journey. It gave me perspective and certainly taught me that what doesn't kill you makes you stronger. I wouldn't be writing this book if I hadn't had those experiences and likely would not have been as successful or worked as hard as I did to rise so quickly in the professional world, reaching executive status in less than 15 years. I say this because this is YOU — for a kid growing up in the system, you've gone through so much, you've had to survive, forget childhood, you have likely lived each day just to make it to the next. In all that, you have been given the gift of street smarts.

Combine your street smarts with formal education and I promise you, you will be unstoppable because you have something that so many others don't. However, you also must make the right choices to cultivate your relationships and education so that you can prepare yourself for opportunities later. I didn't become an executive by skipping school and not doing my homework. I became an executive because I valued learning, honing my skills, and preparing myself for tomorrow's opportunities.

Remember, you are the leader of your life. The decisions you are making today are going to affect you for decades to come. Take your education seriously and use it to supplement the street smarts you've gained due to the circumstances you've been born into. Use these as opportunities for growth and set aside the *poor-me* attitude. I promise, self-pity will get you nowhere; have the mindset of positivity and growth and it will set you up for the life you are destined to have. There will be forks in the road, choices you'll have to make, and how you prepare yourself will determine your destiny. Which road will you take? Choosing a growth mindset and not letting others determine your outcome will take work. Focus on making the right choices with the right mindset and that will put you on the right trajectory to fulfill your life's purpose.

Mandy French
www.mandyfrench.com

Secret *Three*

GIVE IT YOUR ALL

The only place where success becomes before work is in the dictionary.
– Vidal Sassoon,
Hair Stylist and Businessman

If you do nothing, nothing will happen. If you do something, something will happen.

Using your growth mindset to make a choice that will support your vision for the future will now require effort to move it forward. There is nothing you can do in life that will not require work. Effort equals work and it is the key to launching yourself to the next level. If you can embrace work and put in the effort to get results, I promise you will come out on the other side better off that you started. As a foster kid there are many variables working against you; this is why so many kids end up a statistic. If you can master making good choices and then put effort behind how to get from point A to point B (we will talk about goals in the next secret), there is so much opportunity that will open up for you. When you have nothing and can unveil how you have walked through fire to crawl your way out of your circumstances, people will flock to give you a hand up. Not a handout, but a hand up. Effort and hard work are the key elements that glue the secrets to success together.

I want to revisit where you are putting your effort. Is the effort you are exerting giving you results and moving you in the direction you want to go? I have watched, as a foster kid aging out of the system and as a leader at all levels of an organization, how misplaced effort can be incredibly counterproductive. Just because you're putting effort into something, doesn't mean it is the "right" something. The effort you choose to exert is going to determine the type of outcome or pay-off you're going to get. For example, selling drugs, or participating in other illegal activities, is likely going to lead to consequences that can have lasting effects on your future. You might be making money or have earned respect from a gang of friends who admire you, the hard truth of it is the risk is too great. Ultimately, you could get arrested and go to jail, become addicted to drugs, and set yourself on a trajectory of destruction that only leads to more hurt. Not just for yourself, but for the people around you. Similarly, if your perspective seeks out the negative side in every situation (i.e., glass half-empty) and all your energy and effort focus on what isn't going right versus what is, your effort is lost. Remember, negative draws negative.

If you expect life to be dreary and disappointing, it will be. If you expect your circumstances not to change, they won't. However, if you're willing to focus and change your mindset, it will get you on the path for a successful tomorrow. Use your effort and energy wisely to drive you in the right direction. To accomplish this, it starts with discipline. I am pretty sure that as a kid the only discipline I truly understood was when I did something wrong. The consequences of my actions, *blah, blah blah* — but something I learned later is how discipline isn't necessarily what is done to you but what you can train yourself to do. Discipline is the repetitive actions you take to accomplish a goal.

Discipline

Discipline is the first element to driving your effort in the right direction. This goes back to embracing delayed gratification. Understanding that discomfort today will lead to a desired outcome tomorrow. Discipline is what enables you to build the endurance to reach the top of the mountain, build up muscle to lift heavy at the gym, achieve high marks on school assignments, and so on. Understand that you cannot accomplish these things in one day (or one try), it takes effort, commitment, and discipline.

Have you heard the story of the farmer who could lift his 1200-pound cow? When asked how it is possible that he could lift that much weight, he said, "I would lift him every day from when he was a calf and each day, he would get a little heavier and I would get a little stronger." Had the farmer not had the discipline to pick up the cow every day, he would never have had the strength to lift the cow at full-size. In the same way, you must have discipline and repeatedly make choices that are aligned to your goals, even if the desired outcome takes time.

Having discipline is about taking control of a choice or direction you want to go and making it happen no matter what. Make the right choices, day after day, time after time, and work toward achieving your goals or a specific outcome. This is hard, it will challenge you. The secret is keeping yourself accountable to make hard choices that often have delayed outcomes. In time, you'll have the ability to stay focused when temptation and making an impulse decision feel enticing and fun. I also want to acknowledge you have the additional variable of living in a world where you are just trying to survive – this sort of discipline and self-control is tough. This is not a skill that many are born with, it is a skill that you must work at and cultivate; you need to be willing to grow and learn.

Discipline is about mindset, time management, and giving yourself small wins to keep you motivated on the journey. Understand that often, especially when you're young, the discipline you practice today may not have a clear outcome, it is preparing you for future opportunities. As a young person you need to grow your abilities, meaning, build tools and skills to get new outcomes tomorrow.

Make the choice every day to put positive effort into everything you are doing. Figure out what brings you joy or what you're good at and exert your effort in that direction. Find something that fills your time constructively. It is always easier to practice discipline if you are surrounding yourself with people who are doing the same. Get involved! Join a sport, a club, get a job. These are all spaces where you find like-minded people committed to their goals. When you are doing things with other people, it is easier to stay accountable and continue to improve yourself.

When I was 17, I moved to a new foster home in Owatonna, MN, about 90-minutes away from the town I grew up in. I was a junior in high school and transitioned from a very small town, my graduating class no more than 70 or 80 kids, to a much larger town where I was joining a graduating class of hundreds of kids. I went from knowing everyone to knowing no one, a pivotal moment in my life – a moment many of you have felt, probably more than once. The moments when you feel the weight of your life's reality so heavy on your shoulders, the very real feeling of how different you are, how alone it feels to be a foster kid. The crossroad of the next chapter so visible, so raw.

I recall my first day as I walked into that huge school feeling apprehensive, nervous, and alone. I wondered what life would look like, how I would fit in, and who would welcome me. My foster mom, Bev, and I made our way to the administration office to register me for classes, transcripts in hand. The administrator, I don't know if he was the principal or not, welcomed us, nodding at Bev. It was obvious they knew each other, and it wasn't the first time she had brought a "new" foster kid to the school. They shook hands and she handed him my transcripts from my previous school. He looked at her, his eyebrow raised, a surprised look on his face that quickly turned to a satisfied nod and half smile. She said, *"I know, what a nice change, she has so much potential."* They were used to kids in the system who were failing, weren't putting effort into their education, and had given up on life – not engaged, at least not engaged in the right things. That wasn't me. I was committed to hard work and learning. It paid off. In that moment, I felt encouraged, proud, and it gave me confidence to keep moving forward. I was doing the right things, and it was recognized.

When you are disciplined and put effort in the right places, you will begin to get a natural high from the success that you feel. Your brain will literally release endorphins and you will become addicted to success, addicted to that feeling of accomplishment, the feeling of making a difference – helping the people around you to recognize how hard you are working. This is a key element of what has kept me moving forward my whole life. The feeling I get when I can accomplish what others haven't. When I can take my energy and turn my pain into purpose. It excites me and drives me to want to do more. Consider what might happen in your life if you became addicted to success — it feels good, and this is what will catapult you into the tomorrow you envision.

Perseverance

The discipline you practice will get you far; however, it's important to understand there will be setbacks. Not every action or intention is going to go right. Having the ability to push forward and persevere in moments of adversity is a key element to fully capitalize on the effort you are exerting. I would argue that because of your life experience, your perseverance and resolve is greater than most. You have likely not been given much and have had to work hard just to survive and overcome abuse, abandonment, and trauma. Maybe you are already working to overcome poor choices in your past. In any case, you have built remarkable resilience that allows you to persevere, to keep going.

Perseverance is a choice and is a critical part of the growth mindset you've adopted. Understanding life isn't always going to work out the way you want it to, is a reality we all have to face (as foster kids, we know this better than anyone); but more than that, it's about understanding that challenging times help you to build skills and gain tools that will assist you later. Giving up and/or giving in to what is easy (or feels good in the moment) can have devastating effects on your life. Keep your eye on the end game – your vision of what life could become. When you hit roadblocks, keep going – and going, and going, and going, don't stop. Just put one foot in front of another.

Whether you age out of the system, get adopted, or return to your biological family, the struggles of your childhood never leave you. Your family of origin circumstances don't change. It doesn't matter if you are on the childhood or adult side of your life, these are circumstances you can't control and from which you can't run. There is a lifetime of healing and choice ahead of you. During my time in Washington D.C., I engulfed myself in work. I got into a space where I *lived to work* instead of *working to live*. This helped me get ahead in my professional life, but my personal life suffered. I struggled with balance, living a healthy lifestyle – lots of happy hours and eating out. I was tipping the scale at over 190 pounds and was recovering from ending a relationship that devastated me. Once again, I felt alone and, in many ways, out of control of my life. It was time for a change.

In the days that followed, I decided to do something different and go somewhere new. I knew I had to take control of my personal life and take care of myself spiritually and physically. I realized that my perspective changed in all the intervals in my life where choices intersected with a change in geography. Seeing my life and my life's circumstances from different lenses. I needed this change so I started looking at places I would be willing to go to and made a list. Working for the VA meant there was no shortage of opportunity, especially since I was willing to move. Salt Lake City, Utah, made my list. I had gone there for a site visit the year before and fell in love with its beauty. When a job became available there, I found myself moving my life (in reality, it was just my cat, Tux, and me) to this spectacular city, surrounded by mountains, a place only possible by God's hand. With this move, I knew I needed to make changes and practice discipline. I began working out and eating right, no one had ever taught me how to live a healthy lifestyle, so I had to teach myself. I also began hiking regularly.

The mountains in Utah are beautiful, but they are steep. You are hard pressed to find a trail that isn't difficult. I quickly learned the physical meaning of perseverance – literally taking one step at a time to climb a mountain. Desolation Lookout Trail was the first hike I ever did, and I thought I was going to die as each switchback got me closer to the top. I remember taking so many breaks to catch my breath, watching as people passed me on the trail. I continued forward, one step at a time. As I sat on a rock contemplating not going any further a voice ahead of me said, "You're almost there. You've got this!" I looked up and replied, "Thanks!" I took a deep breath, stood up, and kept going. I got to the top that day. It was hard, but the mountaintop view was breathtaking. Sprawled below me was the city surround by the mountains and the valleys. It was a visual reminder of how far I had come, and I embraced the physical exhilaration of having made it. Up to that point, I persevered in so many other ways, but the physical ability to climb this very real mountain was impactful. That was the first hike of the season and I continued to explore Salt Lake City's incredible mountain trails all summer. At the end of the season, I went back to the Desolation Lookout Trail, and I didn't just hike it, I conquered it. I didn't need to stop for breaks, I didn't contemplate turning back and not reaching the summit, I sprinted up that mountain. My grit and perseverance paid off.

Whatever your mountain – whether it is an actual mountain or a situation you must get through, acknowledge the situation and keep going. Persevere because the view from the top is worth it! And remember, the next time you get to climb it – you'll be more prepared. Humans are a unique species. We have an amazing ability to adapt and change both our mental and physical selves. Stretch yourself in all areas of your life; with growth comes discomfort, but it also comes with exhilaration!

Performance

Capitalizing on the effort you exert is also about showing up every day to do the best you can in whatever you are doing. When you put in the bare minimum effort, you will get the bare minimum result. If you want a life of success and abundance, you must put in the work to get noticed. You don't get opportunities or promotions in your career by skating. You get noticed by mastering the role you're in and doing a little more, e.g., staying a little late and learning the why and how of what you do. Learn the job and then innovate, how can you do it better? Never become complacent.

Another way to describe performance is work ethic; I would describe this as the quality and output of the product you're trying to produce. Whether it be your schoolwork, washing dishes at a restaurant, line cook at a truck stop, or leading a government organization (I've done them all) you must take pride in the work you do. Strive to be the best. Strong work ethic will separate you from others and will begin to attract opportunity. Do not show up for a job, do the bare minimum, and get through the day; no, take pride in your work whatever it is. Your work ethic reflects who you are.

As a foster kid, I didn't have a mom and dad who just gave me money. I didn't have the luxury of expensive clothes or the latest technology and toys. I had hand-me-downs, a radio to listen to music, and an allowance. My foster mom gave us an allowance of half our age each week if we completed all our chores. But we couldn't just complete the chores, they had to be done right or we had to go back and do it again. If I wanted extra money to go to a movie or buy something extra, her going rate was $5 per hour to do chores. I remember scrubbing baseboards and walls, organizing closets, dusting and cleaning the bathrooms. I remember how much I hated this and how much I resented not being normal and not having a mom that could just give me the money. Despite my hatred, it taught me the value of a dollar and the importance of saving the money I earned. It was the inception of the work ethic I have today.

In my young teenage years, I played volleyball and basketball. I was never really that good at sports, but it kept me busy, focused, and helped me learn teamwork. As soon as I could start making a real paycheck, I dumped the sports and started making money. My first job was washing dishes at the age of 14 — the earliest possible time I could work. When I was 15, I started waitressing, and then transitioned to a grocery store (stocking shelves and cashiering). I was always a good employee; I took as many hours as they would give me. I was dependable, showed up on time, didn't call out sick, and was willing to work extra shifts if they needed me. My employers always appreciated me and my willingness to do the job and do it well. I genuinely valued getting that paycheck every two weeks and always put half of it in my savings account. I now had the freedom to buy the things I wanted, and it made me feel less isolated, less different.

When I moved to a new foster home at 17, I started working at the local grocery store since I already had experience in the industry. I quickly made a name for myself as I was willing to put in extra effort, provided great customer service, and was dependable. The manager of the store pulled me aside right before the summer of my senior year of high school and explained that they were down personnel on the overnight shift and asked if I'd want to do overnights 11PM to 7AM stocking shelves. I would get night differential pay (a big motivator for me) and if I was willing to do it upon the completion of the summer, they would transition me to the customer service counter and give me the opportunity to be a front-end manager. Wow! What a great opportunity. With the support of my foster parents, I began working the night shift.

In college, although I was awarded a full ride scholarship, I still had to survive and "keep up with the Joneses'" so to speak. Most of the kids I went to school with had mom or dad's credit card, a brand-new car and the best "things". I drove a clunker-1995 Ford Tempo which I bought at the age of 17 for $1500. I paid for my own gas and car insurance. I worked three jobs. Most weekends, I went home to work at the grocery store. I also worked in the admissions office on campus and did odd jobs for people I met in town, e.g. cleaning houses or helping with yard work. Anything to get a few extra dollars, all while going to school full time and getting good grades.

Leaning in and working hard is something I have always done. I developed a consistent and strong work ethic that has launched me from foster kid to executive. I don't know how to do anything "half-assed". I put my passion and my reputation into everything I do – being dependable, showing up, and raising my hand to do the extra things, even when it means self-sacrifice (like working overnight). And just for the record, I would never want to do that again! It was hard to be up all night, sleep all day, and still try to socialize and have a life. But I was motivated to do better, to reach my goals, and crawl out of my circumstances. There was no way I was going to become my mother. There was no way I was going to struggle the way so many did. I was going to make it and it didn't matter how hard I had to work to do it... and that is exactly what I did. My hard work got me noticed and gave me opportunity (we will discuss this further in Secret 6).

I tell all of this to you because I want you to understand that going from foster kid to executive was not a path of luxury – it was a path of hard work and immense effort. It took discipline, perseverance, and high performance. It was *all* the hard work I did throughout my life that prepared me for the professional world and effective decision making to achieve my goals. I used my abilities and work ethic to climb the corporate ladder and I did it quickly. For people who have been given everything, the transition to the professional world can be much more difficult. Remember, hard times prepare us for our purpose. They build the skills we need for success. Adversity is a gift. As much as I wanted to be given that $20 to go to the movies, the 4 hours of work I underwent for 90-minutes of fun taught me the value of time, money, and hard work. Don't shy away from working hard at everything you do. It is teaching you how to be successful and giving you the tools you will need later.

Secret *Four*

PAVING THE WAY

Your goals are the roadmaps that guide you and show you what is possible for life.
— Les Brown,
Politician and Motivational Speaker

Finding your way from foster kid to executive isn't a straight path from A to B. There is an incredible amount of work and planning that goes into having the knowledge, skills, and abilities to achieve that type of success. Getting to executive level takes intention, forethought, discomfort, and perseverance. To truly pave the way, you must understand, embrace, and live the goals you set for yourself. When you reach one goal, it's about setting the next goal even higher. You must believe in yourself and believe you're worthy of rising above your circumstances. Do it for you, but also do it for future generations, for your children and their children. Don't let yourself become a statistic; plan, set goals, and reach them.

What Are Goals?

Goal (noun): The object of a person's ambition or effort; an aim or desired result.

Goals take your choices, mindset, and effort and drive them in a direction that will give you results. Being goal oriented and intentional in your actions is a life skill that will forever serve you and help you reach heights you never knew possible. Often, when speaking about goals, you'll hear the term SMART goals. Goals that are Specific, Measurable, Attainable, Realistic, and Timely. Make your goals specific and narrow, so you can focus on particular areas of interest or need in your life. You want to be able to measure your goals: What does success look like? How will you know you've reached your goal? Ensure that your goal is attainable, and you can specify how you are going to accomplish it. Your goals should be realistic; you should have the ability to achieve them, even if it stretches your abilities. They must fit within your available resources. Finally, a goal should have a target end-date to have achieved results.

Many goals are organically created and become drivers for success; however, being intentional about goal setting drives consistency and success. If goals are not written down, analyzed, measured, and reviewed frequently they are less likely to build self-discipline, help you develop delayed gratification, and drive positive habits. Having SMART goals will give you the results for which you are looking. Be intentional in your development and growth so goals can lift you out of your circumstances for a brighter, more successful tomorrow. Continuous goal setting will allow you to create the habits and milestones you need to reach your vision of the future. You have the ability to do anything you want if you commit and take it one step at a time. We live in the most incredible country in the world, a country that allows you to go from foster kid to executive, but no one can do it for you. *You* must be the driver of your success. Be intentional on your journey to grow; make the right choices every day, have a positive mindset, and put in the hard work.

Goals Create Results

As I mentioned before, I made up my mind at an early age that I wanted to be a lawyer. I'm not sure what first inspired me to say that, but I remember the day it came out of my mouth. I was at church, maybe 9 or 10 years old, and someone asked me what I wanted to be when I grew up. I replied, "I am going to be a lawyer," with conviction. From that day forward, it was my long-term goal, and no one was going to stop me. This goal guided me throughout my childhood to make the small choices every day that would support my dream of being a lawyer. I did well in school, not because I was smart, but because I put in the effort. Doing my homework, always reading books, showing up every day to learn.

When I moved foster homes at the age of 17, I relayed this goal to my new foster mom. I added that not only did I want to go to college, but I was determined to go to one of the private liberal arts colleges in Minnesota. I wanted the same opportunities and education as the "normal," wealthy, privileged kids. If they could do it, why couldn't I? I didn't think about the cost of school (which was over $100,000), or who was going to pay for it, I just saw it as the next step on my journey. Bev, my foster mom, was incredible; she never discouraged me, she never "managed my expectations", she let me dream. She understood the importance of believing in something with your whole heart, with everything you have. She understood that no matter what the outcome my perseverance and drive were more important, more powerful than putting limitations on my dreams of success and normalcy.

The summer after my junior year of high school, Bev took me to all the private colleges in which I was interested. We traveled all around the state to visit schools during a weeklong open house hosted at each college. The last school we were touring was Gustavus Adolphus College in St. Peter, MN. There were around 10,000 residents in St. Peter. Bev grew up only a couple towns over, and she said, "We can go to Gustavus, but you're probably not going to like it; snobby people go to Gustavus." Ha, it's all about perspective. I toured the campus, sat down with the dean of admissions, and learned all about the culture and opportunity this school offered. I walked out of that building, looked over at Bev and said, "This is where I'm going to go to school. It feels like home, it feels like where I belong." Once again, my unsung hero of a foster mom didn't try to change how I felt, she simply replied, "Well, let's get started on your FAFSA applications and applying for scholarships." She gave me 100% support.

A week later, I received a call from my social worker (another unsung hero in my life). She had found a scholarship; it was a full ride to Gustavus. What were the chances?! One of the scholarship criteria was having been a youth in the Big Brothers Big Sisters Program. It had been a long time, but when I was about 5 years old, I had Big Sister – I met the criteria. Now I had to win it. I completed the application and wrote an essay for how being a part of Big Brother Big Sisters Youth Mentoring Program helped me on my journey. Shortly thereafter, I got the news; I had won a full ride scholarship to Gustavus Adolphus College worth over $100,000. Along with tuition, the scholarship paid for my meal plan and housing. The only thing I was responsible for was the required textbooks. WOW! But now I had to be admitted to the school. I completed the application, wrote the admission essays, and submitted my ACT scores – it won't surprise you to learn that I applied for early admission. Gustavus is a prestigious school and my hard work during high school was rewarded, because I got in – the trajectory of my life changed forever, and it started with the dream of being a lawyer. This dream turned into a long-term goal and through the accomplishments of many short-term goals and daily commitment, awarded me the break I needed to launch my future success – and I was ready for it.

Although I'm not a lawyer today, that same goal kept me focused while in college. I needed to do well in my undergraduate to get into law school. I didn't always make the right choice, and there were times where I found myself in situations that could have ruined everything I worked for; it was this goal that kept me focused. It made me get up and show up every day, whether it was to go to work or go to school. It didn't matter if I was out late or didn't feel like it, I knew that I could only depend on me. There was no safety net, if I didn't do it, no one would.

A new opportunity presented itself after college and I landed a job with the federal government. My goal of becoming a lawyer prepared me for this choice. That is what the three-pronged goal approach does, it prepares you for opportunity later; it puts you on the right trajectory for success. Goals give you purpose and purpose drives success.

I believed deeply I was more than the labels and the circumstances I was born into. I believed I could do more and be more. I didn't find all the reasons why I *couldn't*, I found all the reasons and ways I *could*. I didn't blame anyone for my circumstances. I didn't hate others for what they had, I aspired to have for myself. I made the right choices, did a lot of after-action reviews, kept a positive mindset, and worked hard. I did it because I had a plan, I had goals.

Remember, goals are made of choices, mindset, and effort. Taking these ingredients and intentionally using them to move forward is what will make the difference. A dream without a plan is just hope. Don't leave your future to chance; take intentional steps each day to drive you towards your vision for success. Small choices add up.

Having goals is important, but having the right goals is even better. True success and happiness are found when you hit the trifecta of physical, mental, and spiritual health. Goals should be short term and long term. Short term goals include establishing daily and weekly targets that don't just focus on one area of your life but also help you move towards the trifecta of happiness. Like a three-legged stool, if one leg is too short, too long, or missing, the balance of the stool is off or may completely fall over. Balancing your efforts comes with daily habits which will ensure your stability and improve your life. You will also be able to better manage the progress of your goals, discover success, and ultimately find happiness.

Physical Health – taking care of and respecting your body. This is regular exercise, creating activity habits, learning about nutrition and balanced meals. It is also about how you present yourself, the clothes you wear, the make-up you apply, the amount of skin you let others see, or how clean you are. This may also be the piercings and tattoos you have or are thinking about getting. Remember, how you are perceived by others is going to affect the path to your success whether you think that's fair or not. Take time now to build the healthy habits, mindset, and appearance that will support your vision of the future and create physical health for a lifetime. Examples of physical health goals:

- 30 min of exercise or activity per day
- Join a club or sports team.
- Get 7-8 hours of sleep.
- Eat more plant-based foods.
- Achieve or maintain a healthy weight.
- Be free of dependence of cigarettes, vaping, marijuana, other

illicit drugs.
- Drink more water throughout the day.
- Drink 12oz glass of water each morning when you wake up.
- Cut down on processed sugar.
- Create a food or exercise journal.
- Dress up to feel better.
- Learn how to appropriately apply make-up.
- Get a new hairstyle.
- Stretch daily.
- Remove piercings.
- Get outside daily.
- Brush your teeth twice daily.

Mental Health – taking care of your emotional, psychological, and social well-being. This is creating mindfulness activities that help you be more positive, build your brain power, manage your trauma and behaviors, and create meaningful relationships. What we put into our minds and the people we associate with are huge indicators of our success (or lack of success) and mental wellness. Be aware of how you are taking care of yourself and make choices every day that support the life you want. Examples of mental health goals:

- Limit screen time.
- Focus on repairing relationships.
- Journal negative thoughts/behaviors – learn your triggers and learn to intervene before they happen.
- Create a gratitude journal.
- Recite a positive affirmation every morning.

- Be honest.
- Read a book for fun.
- Set aside 1 hour each day, at the same time, to complete your homework assignments.
- Listen to an audiobook on your way to school.
- Listen to positive music – remove negative music from your playlist.
- Journal about your day
- Make a list of the things you like about yourself and read it every day.
- Remove negative people/influences from your circle of friends.
- Learn a new hobby or skill.
- Develop a morning and/or night-time routine.
- Seek out support from a counselor or therapist to talk about your mental health.
- Do SAR mental after-action reviews (SAR = Situation, Action, Result)

Spiritual Health – connecting with your sense of self, others, nature, and God (or other spiritual deity), is achieved when you feel at peace with life. It is finding hope and comfort even when life isn't easy and the season of life you are in is hard. Spiritual health gives you purpose and hope for the future.

- Join a religious youth group.
- Read a devotional or spiritual book each night before bed.
- Volunteer at your church, community food bank, park, animal shelter or non-profit organization (pick an activity that

is meaningful to you) – bonus if you bring a friend.
- Set a dedicated time each day to pray and/or meditate.
- List positive thoughts you want to think about.
- Spread kindness, one act of kindness each day.
- Help someone in need.
- Let go of things you can't control.
- Be forgiving.
- Spend time alone.
- Make a list of encouraging words you can say to someone else.
- Take a chore or activity you don't like and turn it into an act of thankfulness and worship.
- Show empathy to others – put yourself in their shoes.
- Connect with nature.
- Watch motivational speeches.
- Recite a mantra each day.
- Declare your intentions each day (e.g. I intend to be patient, kind, honest and present today).

Goal Setting

I want you to think back to secret one where you developed and proclaimed your dream and vision for the future. Getting from point A to point B is not an easy path, especially under your circumstances, but I still want you to think of some milestones that could reasonably get you to your vision. As you're thinking about those milestones, I am going to share the secret to reaching your dreams: have a plan. Consider your plan for when you're no longer in the system. A moment you may be dreaming about and dreading all at the same time. This is the moment you will have to do things on your own. To figure out how to go on alone. This will be challenging, but remember, you've gone through hard things before, so just take it one step at a time. That is why having a plan and making goals is critical to your success. Even if you're "alone", based on society's definition (i.e., no parents or benefactors to make the transition from childhood to adulthood easy), the choices you have been making, the small habits and short-term goals will help create a community around you; a village that will be inspired to help you and bring awareness of resources that will help build your success. Remember, adversity is a gift and the struggles of today will give way to an easier, more successful tomorrow. Never focus on what you don't have, focus on what you do have – always look forward, never look back. Remember, every "no" and failure leads to "yes" and success in time. It is about mindset; learn from your mistakes, shake them off, and keep moving forward.

Let's put this into practice and work on goal setting using the three-pronged approach – long-term goals, short-term goals, and daily/weekly goals.

Long-term Goals

First, getting a high school diploma (or GED) is not negotiable. You will set yourself up for a much more difficult road if you don't do this. This is your first milestone. The second is what will you do once you graduate from high school – what is your plan? Is it going to a technical school, community college, or 4-year college/university? Perhaps it is an apprenticeship, or joining the military? *You* must choose, you *get* to choose. Getting an education or building a skillset is an investment in your future and part of the success you want to achieve. If the plan isn't yours and you're not invested, it's more likely you won't put the work and effort into being successful. You have to believe so deeply that there is no other way to think, there is no other road to take. Remember my story; know your worth, your dreams hold value and merit – you can do it! You're no stranger to hard work, dedication, and learning – be ambitious – these are marketplace gems that will take you far in whatever endeavor or industry you choose to enter. Succeeding will give you security, which then allows you to move out of survival mode and enjoy this beautiful life you've been given.

Take some time to brainstorm your long-term goals based on your vision/dream statement from Secret one; write it down, proclaim it, believe it deeply, and be ready to live it. What do you want your profession to be? What education or training will you need to get that profession? How much money do you want to be making when you turn 30?

_____

_____

_____

_____

_____

_____

_____

_____

_____

Mandy French
www.mandyfrench.com

Short-term Goals

Short term goals are a bit more fluid. They are dependent on your circumstances and where you are along your journey. Aligning your short-term goals and milestones to your long-term goals will only help your future success. Your short-term goals should prepare you for the future; you must ensure you are building a foundation of skills and achievements that will allow you to continue moving forward. Your short-term goals should also be preparing you for future opportunity, which is a fancy way of saying, be the best version of you every day, growing, learning, and adjusting to your circumstances. Put your best foot forward to show you are invested in your future. This will allow others to see you and they will want to invest in your future as well.

Examples of short-term goals may include passing a difficult class at school, getting your driver's license, buying a car, saving $__ amount of money for a down-payment on an apartment, asking for an informational interview from someone in your desired profession, applying for scholarships, reading one book per month, volunteering, or tutoring youth. Whether it's a milestone in the direction of your long-term goal, or building a life skill for your toolbox, your short-term goals should be unique to your journey.

Take some time to brainstorm some short-term goals.

_____
_____
_____

I recommend revisiting your short-term goals every 1-3 months. Celebrate what you have achieved and reflect on what you have learned using your mental after-action review. Are there adjustments you need to make, or goals do you need to add? Celebrating your successes is important; you are amazing and when you set a goal and achieve it, you deserve recognition and joy!

Daily Goals

Daily goals are the habits you are building to better prepare yourself to accomplish your short-term and long-term goals. These activities will help you, but more importantly they will reshape your behaviors for growth, positivity, and learning self-discipline. Daily goals create structure around your day and help you stay in control of your journey. I recommend small habits that support the trifecta of success; physical, mental, and spiritual health. I use a habit bracelet that keeps me accountable and motivated to reach my daily goals, others use a daily habit journal. Find a mechanism to track your daily goals and keep yourself accountable.

When your daily goals truly become habits, keep them, and find new goals that will continue to enhance your life each day. This is how we become the best versions of ourselves. This is how the tortoise wins the race. This is how YOU win the race! Reminder, goals must be reasonable and attainable; start with one daily goal, something you are intentionally changing and can commit to accomplishing each day.

Use this space to write five daily goals you would like to accomplish and then circle the one you are going to do first:

Be Proud of Your Goals

Congratulations! You are on your way. Writing down goals and being intentional in your actions is the secret to success. To solidify your ability to achieve these goals, look at them each day, declare them out loud, and hold yourself accountable. Be committed. Putting a one-page document together that encompasses all your goals and hanging it up is a great way to keep them top of mind. Visit my website at www.mandyfrench.com/free-gift to find one-page goal templates to make your goal setting easy.

Remember to reflect on your goals, celebrate your accomplishments, and give yourself grace when you need to adjust. Life is full of curves, bumps, and unknown obstacles; adjustments and adaptations are a part of it – don't lose sight of your long-term goal. This is the lifestyle and happiness you aspire to achieve. If you are willing and able, then you are capable of achieving anything to which you put your mind.

Secret *Five*

DON'T DO LIFE ALONE

In the journey of life, it is not where you go, but who you travel with.
— *Unknown*

Don't do life alone. When you're in the system, it is easy to feel like you've been robbed of a family, a childhood, and close relationships. I remember feeling alone often in my youth and as a young adult. The loneliest time of my life was when I had my daughter. It was when not having a mom hurt the most. I felt I should be surrounded by family celebrating this new life, but I was alone. My husband was there, but it wasn't the same. When you are feeling deep aloneness, it is easy to get caught in the "poor me" trap and see what everyone else has as compared to you. However, I've learned to stop comparing myself to others and make the best of my situation. You can too. Remember, you can't change yesterday, you can only change the decisions you are making today that will impact your trajectory tomorrow.

Success doesn't happen alone. While it starts with your individual choices, mindset, effort, and goals, it also takes community, role-models, and mentors (who can be formal and informal). Discovering success is about surrounding yourself with people that will make you the best version of you. They are people who will give you candid feedback, even when it's hard, and people who want to help you reach your goals. I've learned people come and go in your life for a reason, and not everyone is meant to be a part of every season. People are put in your life at certain times that will give you the strength and direction you need to continue moving forward.

Mentors are defined as being "experienced and trusted advisors", which makes it feel like every mentor needs to be old and wise. I am here to tell you that mentors come in all shapes and sizes and the most critical of mentors are the peers and friends with whom you associate. These are the people that will influence you the most (good or bad) and act as informal mentors. The circle of people you choose to surround yourself with is a critical indicator of your own success. You will also encounter formal mentors who are placed in your life to help guide you through formal/professional experiences. They can help you structure goals and provide feedback or advice. Which leads me to a better definition of a mentor: *someone who can support, advise, and guide you; someone who takes the time to get to know you and supports you through challenges and encourages you towards your goals.*

You Are Who You Hang Out With

Objectively looking at the circle of friends you have is critical. Where are they headed? Do they have goals and plans? Do they support you and assist you in making good decisions to be the best version of you? Keep in mind that no one is perfect, and I know I have made my share of mistakes – you're not necessarily looking for Mother Theresa. However, you should consider if your friends get good grades, show up to school every day, are respectful to authority, have jobs or participate in sports. These are some of the questions you should reflect on and observations to think about. If you discover your friends are making poor choices, how long will it be before you do as well? Maybe you're already rethinking some of your recent choices to ensure you make a good choice (aligned to your goals) next time.

The town I grew up in with my first foster family was very small, the graduating class I was in was probably no more than 70 kids. The school system was split between K-6 and 7-12. There was no middle school, just a hallway dedicated to the 7th and 8th graders. I wasn't a popular kid and had kept the same circle of friends throughout elementary school. That being said, it was such a small school, everyone knew everyone. I was 14 going on 25, thinking I already knew all I needed to know about life. This can be a challenging time for any kid and is amplified when you have a stigma attached to your identity. A label that defines you as different than others. It was at this juncture that I found myself with two groups of friends, each going down different paths. I needed to choose which path I was going to travel. I don't think it is unusual for kids in their early teens to begin discovering their value system, which is why this time is so difficult and so critical. Looking beyond the present to see how the choices you're making today will affect tomorrow, especially when it comes to your circle of friends, is hard, really hard. As a foster child you just want to be accepted, you want someone to care for, you want to feel loved and a part of something. I am here to tell you that just because a group of people are accepting you and making you feel wanted, does not mean they are looking out for your best interest. Level up when it comes to relationships and friends because they will influence your growth, development, and choices. This group of people will immensely impact the trajectory of your life and the success, or lack of success, you will achieve. This is powerful and may be difficult to comprehend but trust me, the choices you are making matter. You have so much more power than you can imagine – the key is making choices that support your vision of the future.

As I contemplated each group of friends, one friend helped make my choice a little clearer. She was in 8th grade and pregnant. Talk about a wakeup call. This was not the path I wanted for myself, and a shift happened. I realized my core values did not align with the decisions this friend was making and I chose to step back from the friendship. One day in the cafeteria, I noticed she was upset – I expect she was processing a lot of emotions herself. More than that, her demeanor was spiteful. I don't remember exactly what I said, or who I said it to, but she came up to me, and smashed a Mississippi Mud

Pie directly in my face. I was a chocolate, whipped cream, graham cracker mess, in front of the whole school. Overwhelmed with adrenaline and embarrassment, I considered my choices; I could throw food in her face, I could hit or push her – *my mind was racing with thoughts and feelings.* With a pounding heart and fists clenched, I took a deep breath, called her a bitch, and walked away to clean myself up. I remember worrying that I would get in trouble because I called her a bitch. I found myself pitying her for the choices she had just made. For me, her actions solidified the reason we were no longer friends. Normal people don't smash Mississippi Mud Pie in someone's face, even if they're mad. That isn't the kind of person I wanted to be and not the kind of person with whom I wanted to associate. The fork in the road is the choice you make when you put *yourself* and *your* future first. Making the uncomfortable choice to walk away from influences that would eventually lead me in the wrong direction was the right choice, even though I was hurt and embarrassed.

Divorcing yourself from friends who do not hold the same value system and goals you aspire to is hard, but necessary. I want you to think about the five closest friends you have and ask yourself if you aspire to be like them? This isn't about how much money they have or the kind of clothes they wear. It's about their character, their work ethic, their drive to grow and become a better person. The right mentors are people who are going to influence you in a positive way. If they're not, you need to consider the impact of your decision to associate with people who are going to lead you to making poor decisions and atrophy your ambition to future success and happiness. I will continue to remind you that *today* is temporary and the decisions you are making now have huge impacts on the life you will lead in the future.

Finding the right crowd is not just about them, it is about you. Are you the person with whom ambitious, goal oriented, and hardworking people want to associate? The road goes both ways. It is more difficult to find like-minded people if you are on the wrong trajectory and not projecting confidence, good work ethic, and good behavior. Finding the right crowd starts with looking at yourself and making the small, and sometimes big, adjustments to your own value system to attract people who want to help you succeed.

Be Observant

One of the many challenges of growing up poor, a foster child, a ward of the state, is knowing how to interact with people from the other side of society. People with money, people who are educated and have important jobs, "normal people." It is hard not to see the "them and us" in the situation. It is easy to envy and desire what they have and, in the same breath, fear that world. Fears can manifest differently for everyone; *am I interacting right? Do I fit in? Do I belong? Am I embarrassing myself?* Do not let fear keep you from moving forward because fear leads to blame. You might find yourself thinking about how your circumstances are someone else's fault and you cannot overcome it. In my opinion, fear of the things you don't have is a main cause of generational poverty, addiction, and dependency on the government. Own your circumstances and have the power to lead your own life. Do not let the fear of what others think keep you from escaping. You are amazing in your own right and bring so many incredible perspectives and experiences to the table that are invaluable. Instead of fearing what you do not know, use your growth mindset, and learn how to interact in these situations. Remember, you have control of your destiny – you can choose to face fear head-on and overcome it.

Pay attention and observe how people you admire present themselves and engage in conversation. Become a scholar of people and emulate the ones who reflect the type of person you aspire to be. Part of your success relies on the ability to study how others interact and how you interact with others. Consider how you can adjust what you say and how you act to fit into that world. Learn social queues and etiquette. You may discover you're already great at this. With all the adversity and challenges in your past, you have continuously been learning and adjusting to live with different people, personalities, and expectations. It's likely that you made those adjustments without realizing it because you were forced. Now use this ability intentionally to learn to fit into a successful society. In my experience, adapting to change and adjusting your style for other people is difficult for everyone. You have been honing this skill since the day you lost your innocence, growing up part of the system. Use it. It is a superpower gained from this experience.

Observe your friends' parents, teachers, pastors, social workers, sitcom families, anyone who you come across who has attributes you want. Study them and make their behaviors your own. This is useful as you transition into adulthood because you will know how to interact socially. By observing others and preparing to interact in this environment, you will develop confidence and social skills to give you an advantage in the next chapters of your life, both professionally, and personally. Learning what is socially acceptable and how to interact with like-minded people will lead to your future success.

Getting a scholarship and being accepted by Gustavus was a double-edged sword; it was a private liberal arts college with a great reputation for education. It was also very expensive. Most of the kids came from middle to upper class families. Most of them had trust funds, new cars, and didn't need to work. This was their world. I didn't have that kind of support. Five minutes ago, I was a foster kid and was taking my first steps on new territory. I worked 2-3 jobs at any given time, I drove a rusty, old Geo Tracker (you literally had to get in/out through the passenger door because the driver's door was rusting off). It would have been really easy for me to pity myself or get stuck comparing the differences of our circumstances. Instead, I studied the people around me; I considered things like how they interacted, what they said, what was important to them. This allowed me to continue honing my social skills.

My scholarship paid for school and housing during the school year, but there were always three months of the year that I was essentially homeless. I had to figure out how I was going to survive and where I was going to live for three months of the year. The first summer after my freshman year I spent with my best friend from college. Her grandparents let me live in the basement of their house and I worked at her uncle's truck stop diner as a line cook. I made the best truck stop breakfast you could get. More importantly, I observed their family, how they interacted, how they talked, what they did, and how they lived. They were a huge influence on me and my success. Did I make mistakes? Yes, but I learned and evolved who I was to fit into the life I wanted. I will be forever thankful for that friendship, that summer, and her willingness to share her world and her family with me. It truly made a difference in who I am today.

Remember, when you show you can make good choices, have a positive attitude, are willing to grow, and show a strong work ethic, people are more willing to help you. They'll see the disadvantages you come from and will want to give you a hand up. Not a handout – but a hand up. The kindness of people and mentors in my life is the difference between whether (or not) I could have gone from foster kid to executive. Let people help you. I know there have been people who have let you down, disappointed you, left you, but there are so many good people out there willing to help you and be a part of your life. If you're invested in yourself, others will be invested in you too. But a coin has two sides, and if you're on the wrong path (unwilling to work hard and make good decisions, even when they are uncomfortable), it is less likely that others will care about helping you.

Keep in mind each season of life has different mentors, both formal and informal, and not everyone is meant to be in your life permanently. Instead of pushing people away, embrace them until the time comes when they (or you) move on. Don't dwell on it or take it personally when they go, relationships are constantly evolving. Take away the lessons and memories you gained. Be the scholar who studies the people in your life. Take the tools others are using and make them your own. This is essential for your success.

Perception is Reality

As you master the study of other people you also must be keenly aware of how other people react to you. This is called emotional intelligence and is very important in your journey to success. Being able to "read the room" (which is observing emotions, thoughts, and opinions of a group) and know *when* and *how* to say something is critical. Our behavior, actions, and reactions come from emotion; and emotional intelligence is being aware of our own emotions to recognize and understand the emotion in others. This starts with self-awareness. By understanding your strengths and weaknesses, you'll be able to recognize and observe them in others. It will help you relate to different situations in which you find yourself.

Emotion is powerful and you must find a way to focus your energy and emotions. Use emotion constructively and in a way that enhances, rather than hinders, relationships. Find the synergy between your head and your heart. Sometimes our first reaction and observation get clouded because we are seeing it from a lens of emotion instead of objectively looking at the situation. When you are interacting with others in any situation, ask yourself these questions.

- How are others reacting to what you're saying?
- What are their body language and facial expressions?
- How does what you're saying affect the people around you?
- What value are you bringing to the conversation?
- How are you painting yourself? Meaning, are you being negative and complaining or positive and solution oriented?
- Are you making assumptions?
- Is now the appropriate time to make that joke or comment?
- Are you engaged in the conversation?
- What is your body language and how are people reacting to it?
- What values or emotions do the people you're talking to hold?

You hold a lot of power when it comes to conversation and engagement of others. The secret is understanding how your interactions affect others. Every situation is an opportunity to learn and hone your skills, so if you say something wrong or create an awkward moment, learn from it. Put it in your toolbox and do it better next time. Eventually you will be an expert at not just reading people, but reading a room, and understanding how what you say and do is affecting the people around you.

Take your emotional intelligence to the next level by learning to see the big picture and anticipate the needs of others. This will help you communicate more effectively, and you'll gain respect. You'll also become extremely valuable in the marketplace where anticipating the needs of your leader or customer will give you a leg-up in your career. You might be wondering what "seeing the big picture" means. It's looking past the events happening "now" (i.e., face value) and understanding what others are trying to accomplish, what they need, how you might play into the situation, and any alternative motives. It's like a puzzle. You have all the pieces in front of you, but you must find where they fit without necessarily knowing up front the actual picture you're putting together. Seeing the big picture and anticipating the needs of others is a key skill and you must hone it.

Be present and intentional in everything you do. Observe how others interact, what they say, how they do it. Observe how others react to you and make critical adjustments as you learn more about yourself and how you interact with others. How do the people around you perceive you and your actions? Are you getting the results you want? If not, adjust. Be a scholar of people and practice your mental after-action SAR reviews. Think critically about truly how you affect each situation and how you can continue to grow as you learn more about yourself and others.

Feedback is a Gift.

Part of not doing life alone and having the ability to use relationships and experiences to better yourself, is being able to take feedback and adjust. Feedback is not just criticism, feedback can also be praise. It is a gauge for how you are doing, what you should continue doing and where you have opportunities to adjust. Just because feedback has a valid purpose doesn't make it any easier to hear, especially when it is constructive. In fact, feedback is very difficult depending on the mindset you are embracing when receiving feedback. I've always liked the saying *the truth doesn't hurt unless it should.* Meaning if the feedback hurts or you're embarrassed by it, it's likely because there is some truth to it, and you have some self-reflection to do. Learn to recognize how you react to feedback. Those with a fixed mindset see feedback as something that defines their abilities versus someone with a growth mindset seeing it as an opportunity to adjust and be better. If your belief system is pointed towards growth and always working to be the best version of you, you will see feedback as a precious gift. Continually remind yourself *and believe* you are not limited by your circumstances, and you can grow out of the life you were born in to.

A first reaction to negative feedback might be met with pushback (e.g., whatever happened isn't your fault, you didn't do anything wrong, or your behavior was justified). Remember, you can't control others, but you can control how you react. Be real and authentic with yourself about what role you played in the situation, and how you can learn from it. One of the biggest differences between successful people and unsuccessful people is taking ownership of their actions. Even if the situation is about someone else's perception, their perception is their reality, and you must consider the outcome from their lens. Ultimately, if someone you trust recommends adjustments, take it seriously. This doesn't mean you are necessarily going to make giant life altering changes in an instant but rather, reflect on what small changes you can make to grow (e.g., your communication, your actions, your attitude, etc.) Adjust your daily habits to encompass these changes. Be intentional so you have intentional outcomes.

Surround yourself with people you trust and ask for feedback, this will make you a better version of yourself, help you to continue to grow, and prepare yourself for future opportunities.

Seek Mentors

When you are being intentional about your future and putting effort into the things you do, people will notice. Teachers, coaches, pastors, employers, foster parents, social workers, friends – everyone with whom you interact. They will notice your investment in yourself and will likely want to invest in you too. We will talk more about this in the next secret as it relates to opportunity, but the key is understanding people are, and will continue to be, placed in your life to help, and guide you. Don't get wrapped around the title of mentor, many people on your journey can be considered mentors but are never actually called that. Simply put, they are the people who are helping to shepherd you on your path. Giving feedback, advice, raising you up, and encouraging you on the way. When you find these people, embrace them.

Having mentors and people who are invested in your success is like having road signs on your path. They help with course corrections, push you to keep going, provide a listening ear, and share in the celebration of your progress. They can also help you process as new opportunities arise. I understand if this concept makes you pause. I was let down a time or two by people I trusted on my journey, but I learned from those moments too. Don't let the past deter you from opening up to people who want to help guide and encourage you. Don't do life alone. Having these people in your life will help you achieve your goals.

If you don't have a mentor, who is your hero? Who do you look up to? With them in mind, when you're in a situation ask yourself, is this what my hero (or mentor) would do? Use role models in your life as guideposts for knowing what to do next. Each season of your life will have different mentors and role models helping you in one way or another. Seek out people you admire and want to be like in each of these seasons. Let them be your anchor to help ground you. You are the best version of yourself when you're surrounded by people who have the attributes, characteristics, values, and experiences that you are striving to replicate.

There have been so many influential people in my life. I definitely didn't get to where I am today alone. What I have found is that the label of "foster kid" combined with the effort I was putting into my future allowed more people around me to notice me and invest in me. They would encourage me, nudge me towards opportunity, give me feedback and help me feel welcome in the space of which I was a part. I can't say there is any one person who had the biggest impact; I truly feel that there was someone in each season of my life that took me under their wing and helped to shape who I am in some way.

I don't talk often about my first foster mom. In short, we had some disagreements while adjusting to my circumstances. Over time, I started focusing less on what didn't go right and more on what I took from the experience. I am who I am because of her. She is a strong woman and impacted many kids. She taught me discipline, consequences, and a strong work ethic. More than that, she allowed me to experience so many different things. She was a powerful mentor on my journey. She raised me to be independent and instilled in me the power of gender equality.

I understand it is hard sometimes to appreciate the foster parents that have been put in your life. I know not everything is great and each situation is different. However, take the goodness from each of them as a gift. It shapes who you are and who you will become. Seek to find the silver lining in every situation. I often learn the most from people who I don't agree with and don't want to emulate (i.e., learning what not to do is still learning). Bottomline, don't let the bad define you, take the good even if it's just a sliver. Another phrase I like is *what doesn't kill you makes you stronger* and these people, whether you like them or not, are shaping who you are becoming.

If you're waiting for that one person who is going to throw you a lifeline, you're likely not going to find it. You must take control and remember there will be many people offering to help you once you commit to your goal. Learn to recognize when others are trying to help you. It may be uncomfortable at first or hard to hear feedback, but it'll get easier the more you practice. Be open to others willing to guide you on your path. These are life's road signs, don't let them go to waste.

Secret *Six*

THE NUDGE

Life has a funny way of nudging you in the right direction.
– *Mandy French,*
Executive, Author, Speaker, Coach

One of the mantras I have experienced and continue to live by is *life has a funny way of nudging you in the right direction*. The universe is full of energy positive and negative and when you are giving off vibes of success, power, and ownership, the universe has a funny way of nudging you in that direction. You don't always have a clear path ahead, or know what the next right move is, you must trust that your ability to visualize what you want will lead to the opportunities that will get you there. That is, if and only if you're willing to say yes, commit, work hard (really hard), and be uncomfortable from time to time. At a certain point, the only thing standing between you and your desired life, is you. If you believe in yourself and focus on your long-term goals while doing everything within your control to build the habits and abilities to support that dream, the universe will reveal the next steps to you. After that, all you need to do is recognize the opportunity when it arises and be willing to take it.

The journey you have taken through this book culminates right here with opportunity. For success and happiness beyond your wildest dreams, you must be constantly practicing all the secrets to success (i.e., choice, mindset, effort, goals, and relationships). This determines the type of opportunity you are going to attract and what becomes available to you. I want to reemphasize the importance of your beliefs and taking ownership of your future. If you are not "all in", neither will be your potential supporters or the universe. Take time to acknowledge your current situation, let go of any notion of being the victim and get started. Remember, your circumstances don't define you or your future. If you live life every day believing in yourself, good things will happen. If you're stuck in negativity, nothing will change.

Remember, adversity is a gift (one of which you've been given a lot). Although it isn't always easy to see the positives of your circumstances, there are advantages. Being a foster kid opens doors that are not available to other people. Take advantage of this and capitalize on the situation you are in; grab all the goodness you can get to launch you forward. There are scholarships, Pell grants, internships, and social services has budgeted dollars to help pay for opportunities. It all comes back to whether (or not) you're willing to invest in yourself. Once you get started, your confidence will build, and this will give others confidence that your trajectory is something they want to be a part of. You're worth it!

People/society want to help you so put those superpowers to use. Show your ability to be a good problem solver, work hard, listen, observe, be resilient, and manage change – these are skills for which colleges, scholarships, and employers are looking. You're a better bet than someone who was handed a silver spoon. In my experience, a common thread amongst leaders is having experienced some sort of adversity or obstacles to get to where they are in life . You've got this kind of experience in spades. Your ability to become an expert in leading your own life will also reflect itself in your ability to lead teams, and (if you want) be a world changer.

Try, Try Again

Resiliency is the ability to keep on moving forward even when faced with failure, disappointment, and adversity. Taking calculated risks, giving something a try, and failing is okay. I give you permission to fail, in fact, I encourage it. Every failure leads you closer to success. Failure shows you a path that doesn't work, so, learn from the experience and try again.

Overcoming failure is all about mindset and understanding it is okay to try something, even if it doesn't work. Know the experience is a part of the journey and not the destination. The definition of insanity is doing the same thing over and over again expecting a different result. If it isn't working, try something different – don't give up.

It's a numbers game. Eventually you will find the recipe that works, and the right combination of events will happen. By this time, you'll be ready for it because you haven't given up and you've learned so much from your experiences. Being resilient will help you stand up when you fall down, brush off your knees, and try again. There is no replacement for trying, no short cuts. The one thing I can promise is that doing nothing will get you nothing, so keep at it and you'll continue to move forward.

The moments of adversity and challenges you have had to overcome, by no choice of your own, have given you a resilient superpower that others don't have. Think about it, you've overcome so much hurt, abandonment, rejection, and change. You've had to keep moving one foot in front of the other despite your circumstances. You understand disappointment. Use these skills that have been forced on you and use them to make you better, enhance your opportunities, and reach your goals. Don't let failure slow you down, let it be a tool that continues to launch you forward. I can't tell you how often people are amazed by how far I've come – the reality is, being on a path to success (i.e., owning the decisions I'm making and choosing to learn from my experiences) is WAY easier than the childhood I had to endure.

I realize I made it seem easy to swallow the disappointment and despair that might come from a failure. That somehow your mind can tell your heart to simply not feel disappointment when failure happens. That's not the case, it is still going to hurt, make you sad or frustrated. Instead of focusing on the negative, you must shift to what's next, so you don't get stuck. It really is as simple as our mental after-action SAR reviews; look at the s̲ituation, what a̲ction did you take, and what were the r̲esults? Then, you'll be able to consider what you learned and what you can do differently to keep moving forward. Nothing is ever lost if you learn from experience. Mastering moments of failure will help build upon your experiences on your path to success.

As I sit here thinking about a story of my own failure, I am having a hard time. Not because I haven't failed – but when I do fail, I don't really label it as failure. In my mind it is just an opportunity to do something different and listen to how life is nudging me to shift my effort. It isn't a failure because I know I've put my best foot forward. I have put my heart and soul into doing a good job and giving it my best effort, so I consider it is just another life lesson to prepare for challenges down the road. It's less about the failure and more about my commitment to keep trying, over and over again. Keep your vision of the future at the forefront of everything you do, and your effort will pay off in time. It is only a failure if you didn't put in the effort, don't seek to understand the result, and don't learn from the experience. Move on and commit to putting in the effort you can be proud of.

The Worst Thing Anyone Can Say to You is No

I have found that one of the residual challenges of my circumstances is sometimes I'm scared to ask for things. Fearful of getting in trouble, disappointing others, not knowing how to ask, someone saying no or rejecting me. I'm here to tell you, kick fear in the face and just ask. The worst thing anyone can say is no and there is always something gained in asking and having the experience no matter what it is.

When I was in college, an incredible opportunity in and of itself, I was given the chance to spend an entire semester studying abroad in India. The cost of a semester of school was the same as going to India for a semester, so I was able to apply my scholarship to this experience and it was incredible. I experienced so much personal growth while in India. It taught me a lot. After returning, I sat with my best friend (she had gone to India as well) and was surprised to find myself in a conversation about traveling for 3-weeks in Egypt during J-term. (J-term is a single class taken in January as part of Gustavus curriculum.) We still had wanderlust of our time in India and experiencing different cultures. [Quick tangent, seeing the world is powerful and if you get the opportunity, I highly recommend it, experiencing different cultures changes your perspective on life.]

Anyway, she came from a well-off family who could afford to fund this adventure, but the $5,000 price tag was way out of reach for me. She said, "Just ask your scholarship foundation, see if they'll fund it." I looked at her like she was crazy. Wouldn't it be selfish of me to ask for more? They're already paying for my premium education; I just spent a semester in India – how could I possibly ask for more? She said, "Mandy, the worst they can say is no. You won't know unless you ask." So, I did (stomaching a combination of fear and butterflies). I remember closing my eyes as I clicked send on the email. The scholarship coordinator called me a couple days later and asked how the J-term class fit into my major. The course was called Ancient Egyptian History, and I was a history major – a perfect fit. She said she would talk to the board and get back with me on a decision. You can imagine my shock when she called back to tell me that they would pay for the J-term experience. HOLY SMOKES, they said yes!

This is a lesson I've carried with me and pass on as frequently as I can. You won't know the answer to something unless you ask, sure they can say no, but what if they say yes? Take the risk of rejection. That is how life springboards you to the next level, a steppingstone. These are the moments that shape who we are and who we are becoming. It can be easy to limit yourself considering your circumstances, but don't do that. Focus on what you can control and what is available, because why *not* you? Be ready to use the resources available to you. Visualize it and draw in opportunities for yourself.

Conversely, try not to get discouraged when an opportunity arises, and the answer is no, or you choose not to take hold of it. It is not about pursuing all opportunities, just the right ones that align to your goals. Remember, there is another opportunity on the horizon that you're not aware of yet. The closing of one door always opens another – just be patient, continue to stay focused and positive and life *will* nudge you in the right direction.

No Regrets

Life is too short to have regrets, which is why every time an opportunity presents itself, you should be present and weigh the pros and cons. Don't let fear of the unknown or the lack of knowing how stop you from taking the right opportunities. Life's nudges are there to help build the skills and abilities you need to level up. Remember, choosing not to choose is also a choice and often when opportunity arises you must be decisive and step outside of your comfort zone. Although this feels hard and scary, I want you to recognize how good you are at this. You've had to do it your whole life – you've faced scary things in many situations, now let that skill work *for* you. Discomfort is temporary, sometimes we have to fake it 'til we make it, which means acting like we know how to do something until we do it.

I have primarily lived my life on the premise of allowing the universe, my God, nudge me in the right direction. Taking opportunity as it is presented and letting life guide me on this journey. I recall a time where I didn't take an opportunity, I was in college and my social worker reached out about an internship she had found working in Washington D.C. with Congress on foster care legislation. There was a simple application process, and I was the perfect candidate. At the time, I was distracted by a romantic relationship and wanted to enjoy the summer making memories with my friends. I thought that was a better use of my time than living in D.C. as an intern for this incredible opportunity. I never filled out the application. Then, I lied to my social worker, telling her I wasn't selected. I felt awful and lied because I was ashamed that I hadn't at least put my name in the hat for the chance to be selected. I rejected this opportunity from the universe, and for what? Fun in the moment... Instead of doing the hard, right thing – I knew better.

I'll never know if I would have been selected for that internship or what other opportunities might have followed, but this choice did teach me that I don't want to live a life of regrets. I don't want to look back and think what if I had just tried, or what if I had just taken the time – what if. From then on, I have lived a life looking out for what's next, so when the universe brings me an opportunity and shows me the direction I need to go, I'm not going to be the one that stands in the way.

You might be thinking, this is silly – you want the universe, God, to tell you what to do? Yes, that is exactly what I'm saying. If you are focused and aligned with your vision of the future and believe that you're capable of accomplishing anything (truly believe), then your dreams will manifest and be delivered to you. You just have to be willing to recognize the right opportunities, take them, and always do your best in everything you do. If you are putting in the effort, you will have the control to make your dreams come true. Trust that opportunities will come. It may not always be exactly what you expect, but it will arrive all the same. If it is meant to be, it will be.

Be open to the universe speaking to you, see the signs (opportunities) that will help you know what the right next step is. You must have faith that the path is already paved for you, and you must be willing to change when life nudges you in a new direction. You deserve this. You deserve to make your dreams come true. Use the secrets of success to attract the right people and get the right opportunities for you. Believe in your future and work hard on relationships, choices, and a mindset that will prepare you at every stage of your journey. If not you, then who? Why not you?

I have a good friend who always gets a little irritated with me when I talk about my success in such a laissez-faire way. When I say things like *life has a funny way of nudging me in the right direction*, or *if it's meant to be, it will be*, she feels like I degrade the hard work I have put into my success and the intentional choices I have made to get where I'm at in life, which is not the case. I know how hard I have worked to get where I am today. I want you to understand that just because you are letting the universe guide you, you are still taking all the secrets talked about in this book and applying them every single day. Remember, doing nothing will give you nothing, and doing something will always get you something. The daily habits you are putting in place will support your choices, enhance your mindset, strengthen relationships, and deliver results. Opportunities will grow and before you know it, you'll realize how far you have lifted yourself up. I believe you can truly manifest the life you want. If I can do it, you can too!

One Last Message: Gluing It Together

Success is not merely the achievement of goals; it's the relentless pursuit of excellence and the ability to turn setbacks into steppingstones.
- Unknown

Anyone can find success if you put the right tools in place and are willing to shift your mindset from *why me* to *why not me*. My hope is that as you've read this book you have been able to identify how you can make small changes today that will cascade into big changes tomorrow. Now, the real question is, how do you take these six secrets and truly allow them to guide your life day in and day out, so you are triumphant? Use the glue – faith, forgiveness, and putting YOU first.

Faith

Faith is believing in something before it is true. The dictionary defines it as "complete trust or confidence in someone or something." The Bible defines it in Hebrew 11:1 "Now faith is the assurance of things hoped for, the conviction of things unseen." Faith is this ambiguous thing that people speak about, but how do you get it? How do you use it? Where do you find it? In my experience, it comes from believing in something bigger than you, a higher power. For me, that is God. I genuinely believe that Christianity played a key role in my youth, and it allowed me to not set limits in my life. I was able to see myself through God's lens and it helped me dream. I have not always been faithful in my relationship with Him, but He has always been faithful to me. Through all my challenges, through all the opportunities and struggles, lonely moments, and poor choices, He guided my path and protected me. He *is* life's nudges that have allowed me to make the right choices to get me to this place. He created the universe, and it is the guiding hand that helps show me the way. He is my truth and beacon.

No matter what you believe, your faith will allow for the limitless possibilities available to you. Faith creates space for you to meditate and will unburden you in times of helplessness. It will give you power to move forward, even when it's hard. Trust that life will nudge you in the right direction, revealing opportunity and next steps on your journey. Having the ability to patiently live through the season you are in and embracing lessons, relationships, and experiences, is the power of faith and believing in a higher power. Believing that the choices and effort you are exerting will truly pay off. I know how difficult it is to have hope and faith when it feels like the world is against you and you've been given the short end of the stick, but faith can deliver you and help you defy the odds.

For the six secrets to work you must have faith that tomorrow *can* be better, and your dreams *can* come true. Despite the hard or harsh reality of today, faith prepares better things for you later. It allows you to rise above and feel the energy around you (positive and negative). Do everything you can to tap into the positive energy around you, truly believe in your vision of the future and your ability to climb out of today's reality. We live in a world where this is possible, and you deserve it!

Each day take the leap of faith (choices, mindset, effort, relationships) and trust that everything will work out the way it is supposed to.

Forgiveness

For those of us that have grown up in the system, we have been hurt in unthinkable ways. If your experience is anything like mine, you've spent years going to therapy, hearing the experts tell you how to deal with your trauma, helping you understand why you are the way you are. You've probably been given a diagnosis. I'm here to remind you, not to let this define you. A diagnosis cannot determine who you will become. You are amazing just the way you are. There's this perception that if you go to therapy and/or take some pills for your mental health, you are going to be, or should be, healed. Like somehow those things are supposed to take away the hurt and the anger. More than that, if somehow you don't connect with your therapist or don't walk out of the office being "normal", you will be forever tainted by the experiences that happened to you. The reality is you can't change the past, and you will never be able to change the experiences that brought you to today. Therapy and other mental health tools can help, but your experiences have made you who you are. To use these experiences in a way that makes your life better instead of being an excuse for not moving forward, you must have the ability to forgive.

Forgiveness is a loaded term and may be difficult to fully understand. In fact, it has taken me years to recognize that forgiveness isn't about the person who hurt me, it's about freeing myself from their actions. Accepting you can't change the past and you can't change anyone (but yourself) will help you truly move forward. At some point, you will have to forgive those who have hurt you. When you hold on to the past it, clouds your ability to see the present moment and see the potential of the future. Without forgiveness, you live in the past with the same emotions.

To forgive, you must have compassion for the person who hurt you. You're probably cursing me right now; how could you possibly have compassion for someone who has done horrible things to you? This might mean compassion for the person who is the reason you don't have a family, or the reason you are separated from your siblings. They might have physically, sexually, or emotionally abused you or made you steal or do other acts of crime – how could you forgive that person? I know how difficult these questions are and what I'm recommending; confronting the root of your hurt, the person or people who have altered your life in permanent ways. Try to imagine for a moment this person as a three-year-old child, looking up at you with big innocent eyes. The person or people you need to forgive were innocent at one point too. They have likely been hurt in their past and carried their hurt while also passing it on to you. By forgiving them (this doesn't mean you will forget), you are releasing their grip on your life.

It took me many years to forgive my mom. Of all the actions that were difficult to understand and to forgive, my mom's selfishness was the hardest. Understanding she was mentally ill and couldn't take care of me or my sisters; she was unwilling give up her parental rights. She unwaveringly picked me up every other weekend to see her. Although this was more than most kids, I never understood why she would rather see me live out my childhood in foster care, rather than live a life of normalcy. This isn't something I focused much on as a kid, but as an adult it was difficult to not blame her for robbing me of a childhood and family that I could have had and wanted. I was eight years old and could have easily been adopted by a nice family willing to give me stability and the normal childhood for which I longed. Instead, I felt like she was only thinking of herself.

Forgiving her and moving on with my life was the most important thing I could have done. In fact, in many ways, my success drew from the simple fact that I was going to be everything she was not. I didn't want to end up alone, struggling, and unaccomplished. It was the summer before my junior year of college, I was 21 and as she laid on her deathbed fighting for her life, I forgave her, and it gave me closure. Now, as a mom myself, I can't imagine how difficult it was for her to have put her three daughters in foster care, acknowledging she didn't have the capability to parent her own kids. I can't imagine the sadness, frustration, and anger she must have felt towards herself and her shortcomings. So, when I say forgiveness benefits you and you'll be able to move on, and focus on what matters, you understand my meaning. Don't let anyone define you. More importantly, don't replicate what you have been shown, break the cycle, and by forgiving them, you are breaking the chain.

Everything happens for a reason; I wouldn't be writing this book if the decision and circumstances of my mom hadn't happened. I wouldn't be the person I am today without all those experiences and my community. I wouldn't change my past; but I wouldn't want to live it again. Because of my journey, I am a million times more thankful for everything I have, my accomplishments, my faith, and my family. Forgiving my mom and so many others set me free and helped make my life better.

Take the steps you need to take to forgive the people who have hurt you. This doesn't mean that they are going to acknowledge wrongdoing, or somehow be a different person; you must forgive them because you want to forgive them. In doing this, you'll free your mind, heart, and soul.

Putting YOU First

I understand that you are dealing with a whole lot in life, and it might be difficult to prioritize YOU. It is okay to put yourself first. It's not being selfish. In fact, it's one of the healthiest things you can do for yourself regardless of your season.

My life has been full of geographic moves, and what I've found is that each move I make gives me a different perspective and lens through which to see the prior chapter. The first time this happened was when I moved back to Owatonna as a junior in high school. Up until this point, my biological mom and I were really close. She always gave me a sympathetic ear and would visit every other weekend. She was committed to having a relationship which was more than many of the other kids I grew up with in the system had. Being bipolar meant she had a lot of mental struggles. I remember when she tried commit suicide when I was in 8th grade and when she bought hundreds of dollars of earrings from Claire's while in a manic state (when she could barely afford rent or food on the table). I remember when she was put in jail because she threatened my foster when she learned she couldn't see me. She called over and over again, and finally showed up at the house uninvited. I remember wanting to take care of her, wanting to protect her, wanting to be there for her. I was a kid. I remember being angry with my foster mom; how could she be so awful to my mom? By extension, she was being awful to me. It's hard to understand mental illness and relationships when you're a kid.

My mom lived a lonely life and I needed to make sure I was there for her. When I was given a choice to move away from the foster home, I did. The relationship dynamics between my foster mom and my biological mom were a big part of that decision. So, it was interesting when I realized, at 17, I had been holding the role of "mom" and caretaker in our relationship. I was enabling her, and she was enabling me. I decided I didn't want to play that role anymore and set some boundaries. If she wanted to talk, she could call me or come by. I set out to take care of me. I was a junior in high school, I had to start thinking about my future.

This approach quickly turned our relationship in a different direction. We talked less and less; she would get angry with me, accusing me of drinking and smoking (i.e., making poor choices). The reality was, I was just trying to be a teenager and learning what it meant to take care of myself. She was mentally ill, and I knew that if all my energy was focused on helping her, I wouldn't be able to make the choices I needed to for me. We talked very little up until when she passed away about four years later from bladder cancer. She was initially diagnosed while I was in high school but had gotten treatment and went into remission. When it came back, she couldn't get healthcare other than emergency care because she didn't have insurance. She still owed the hospital from her previous treatments. An oncologist wouldn't see her until it was an emergency and by then the cancer had metastasized throughout her body. It was too late. In the end, I made sure I was there every day for the last four weeks of her life. I made sure I created the space for the closure and forgiveness we both needed.

If you're not already familiar with codependency, look it up. It's important to not let your reliance on others keep you from moving forward. I don't know if my approach was the right approach, but it allowed me to focus on making the decisions I needed to ensure my life was going in the right direction. Looking out for yourself before others can be looked upon as a negative, but for kids like us, we don't have a family safety net and social structure to support us. If we don't do it, no one will – which is why I'm writing this book. I wish someone could have told me and the other kids in the system with whom I grew up these simple secrets to building a successful tomorrow. For example, knowing that we would need to push through our trust issues to create space for people to give us a hand up would have saved me some time and energy. I am here to tell you that it is okay not to know everything, but only you can make the choices to change your story. You can do anything you put your mind to – if you want, you can go from foster kid to executive, or foster kid to _____, you fill in the blank. The power is in your hands. Your life is yours alone and you have to choose how you are going to live it. Don't let the circumstances of your birth and your family of origin determine your worth and your future. You were put on this earth for a purpose — go out and find it, make a difference, make a beautiful life.

Now, go do it.

It is hard as a young person to let go of today and truly prepare yourself for tomorrow, I know. Especially when you are in survival mode. Most days, you're just trying to get through. But there are reasons the statistics don't play in your favor and you are likely to continue the cycle. We learn what we are shown, so that might be pregnancy at an early age, becoming homeless, drug addiction, physical or mental abuse, sex trafficking, and so on. Maybe your kids end up in the same situation, the same cycle. I want you to leave reading this book with more than hope. I want you to have actual strategies you can put in place to take control of your destiny. Don't let the system or society tell you that you can't or that you won't. Take one step at a time, live each day with intention and kick the statistics in the face. You can do anything you want – so do it, the choice is yours. You are the only one standing between you and the future you want.

You started this book by creating your vision of what your future looks like. You put your heart and soul into how your life might manifest. Read your vision every day, or every week, or, at least, every month. Hold on to what can be if you make good choices, have the mindset of a winner, work hard, and do your best. Build relationships that reflect the type of lifestyle and accomplishments you want. If you do all these things, opportunity will come knocking and success will not be far behind. In time, you will see your dreams unfolding, you will soar above the hurt, shame and circumstance you were born into, and you will change the world. Not just for you, but for your future generations. I believe in you.

Mandy French
www.mandyfrench.com

About the Author

Mandy French was placed in foster care at the age of 8, as a result, she spent a decade navigating the social, emotional, and family challenges of growing up in the system. Using a winning mindset, grit, and perseverance, she crawled her way out of her circumstances through the help of powerful mentors, influencers, and the ability to capitalize on opportunity.

Having received a scholarship to Gustavus Adolphus College where she graduated with a degree in history, she has spent the last 17 years employed at the Department of Veterans Affairs, the second largest federal government agency, working her way into an executive position. After reaching unimaginable success and living a blessed life beyond anything she could have imagined, she has pivoted her career to give back to the community and system she sprouted from.

Understanding she is a part of the top 3% of foster kids who not just aged out of the system but has reached this level of success; she wants to teach youth the key secrets to building a successful tomorrow by taking ownership of their futures and creating the habits that will drive them to break the generational and societal chains keeping them from reaching their full potential. Her goal is to work with this vulnerable population to intervene before homelessness or human trafficking swallows their future and perpetuates their circumstances.

Foster youth are given the gift of adversity, and she is passionate about helping them identify the superpowers that give them an advantage in today's marketplace. She recognizes this comes not only from giving tools, motivation, and inspiration to these kids, but also by providing tools to the caregivers and professionals supporting this population every day.

Mandy French is a transformational speaker, author, and coach on a mission to change the trajectory of foster youth and their future generations. She lives in Phoenix, Arizona with her husband and five-year-old daughter.

Acknowledgments

As I have embarked on this literary journey, I have had the opportunity to reflect on the countless individuals who have been a part of my life's story and helped me along the way. I am grateful for the support and inspiration from so many who have come and gone in the different seasons of my life, all leaving a lasting impact. Their encouragement, wisdom, and unwavering belief in me has shaped the person I am today and allowed me to take on this project and share the secrets I have used to escape the circumstances of my childhood. It is with heartfelt appreciation that I extend my deepest thanks to so many; although, it's impossible to thank everyone, I apologize for anyone not listed, please know I appreciate you greatly.

To my husband, Jim. Thank you for your support, encouragement, patience, and unending love. I am forever grateful for getting to do life with you every day, I could have never imagined the life we have built together; it is truly blessed and beautiful beyond words. I am the best version of me with you, I can't tell you how grateful I am for all you do for our family; I couldn't have done this without you. Love you the most-est.

To my daughter, Evelyn. Becoming your mommy has forever changed who I am, it has given me new meaning to my purpose and my story. You gave me perspective, showed me unconditional love, and helped me heal from the inside out. I will forever do all I can to give you everything I didn't have and everything I did. I love you more.

To my foster mom, Bev. Only a part of my story for a short time before being taken too early from breast cancer, she was truly the unsung hero in my life, she will never know the great heights I have achieved but she will always be the woman who let me dream. She did not let my circumstances or my 'labels' limit who I was, or who I was becoming. She let me bloom and I will forever be grateful for her.

To my foster dad, Jim. Thank you for being my number one fan. Just knowing you were there with a listening ear and helpful hand means the world to me. I didn't ask for help often but when I did you were always there. Thank you for believing in me!

To my foster mom, Mic. Thank you for cultivating me into the strong woman I am today. Although I didn't appreciate it at the time, you gave me the structure and discipline I needed to become the person I am today. Thank you for all you did for me and the countless other kids you impacted over the years.

To my college crew - the girls who accepted me as one of them and taught me more about life than they will ever know. You are my tribe and I love you all - I'm looking forward to dorm life 2.0 at our future retirement home!!

To the teachers, coaches, pastors, social workers, mentors and parents of so many friends who took the time to help me along the way in all the different seasons of my life. Your influence, guidance, advocacy, and kindness made a huge difference in my life; it shaped my worldview and pointed me in the right direction. I notably want to thank my social worker, Marcy Fensky, you were the cheerleader and advocate I needed as I was aging out of the system; to Dennis and Kristin Tuel, thank you for welcoming me into your family and home, there are no words to describe my appreciation for your kindness and generosity, you are incredible people; and finally, my Uncle Brent and Aunt Kris, thank you for your support over the years whether it was giving me a bed to sleep in and an address to direct mail to or being the best Auntie and Uncle Evelyn could ask for, I am incredibly grateful to have you in our lives.

To Al and Cathy Annexstad and the Annexstad Family Foundation. Thank you for changing the trajectory of my life!! Your generosity allowed me to gain not just a world-class education, but it also expanded my horizons both culturally and socially; without access to these opportunities, I would not be where I am today. Thank you for making a difference in so many lives!

To Jesus Christ, my savior. Even when I was not faithful to You, You were faithful to me. Thank you for never leaving my side, protecting me from harm, and nudging me in the right direction time and time again. I owe everything to You.

Special <u>FREE</u> Bonus Gift for You

To help you to achieve more success, there are **FREE BONUS RESOURCES** for you at:

www.mandyfrench.com

Get your Success Toolkit: including your Dream Catcher, Gratitude Grid, Paving Your Path, Habit Trackers and many more worksheets to launch your success journey into *ACTION*.

Made in the USA
Columbia, SC
27 June 2024